drum tongue griotry:
an echoing of ancient beats
books iv, v, vi

a third eye
visions productions

drum tongue griotry:
an echoing of ancient beats
books iv, v, vi

jamal english
as
last ewe griot

Cover Design by Keyra English

Published by a third eye visions productions

First Printing in paperback and ebook in August 2020

The publisher is not responsible for websites (or their content)
that are not owned by the publisher.

Title: drum tongue griotry: an echoing of ancient beats / Jamal D. English

ISBNs: 9798665113234 (trade paperback), (ebook)

Printed in the United States of America

This book is typeset in Skia

libation

mother: i knew you would come
                          knew, if anybody'd come, it'd be you
                          that you'd need, it'd be?   settled—

mother: go'n now—
                          home, where ya b'long—
                          nexta erin—
                          taking care'va my grandbabies!

mother: I remember everything,   way back—
                          just,   not?

mother: gotta—
                          check y'self,
                          b'fore, you check—
                          your babies—

son: rest,   momma
                                        alrightnow—

Donald Byrd's "Flight Time" as requiem
walks momma through
the opening gates

continuation

In 1990, in a club somewhere in Philadelphia, a remixed song saved my father's life. Fingers Inc., "My House"—

> In the beginning, there was Jack, and Jack had a groove, and from this groove came the groove of all grooves, and while one day viciously throwing down on his box, Jack boldly declared, "Let there be HOUSE!" and house music was born.

And then the beginning *dun DUN* of Let's Go by Fast Eddie blared through a hundred speakers, and the stars aligned.

My dad tells me music saved his life. Specifically, house music saved his life. Without it, he wouldn't be here; without it, I wouldn't be here.
He tells me that, when I was born, he played music and that's what made me move. He says that in that moment, he knew music would do for me what it did for him.

If my life was a book, the chapters would be divided by phases of music--the music that made the walls of the house shake with bass or sway with melody. House, Hip Hop, Neo Soul, Rock, Reggae. Even twelve stringed classical Spanish guitar.

I learned how to tell stories not just through the hundreds of books crammed into our dozens of bookshelves, courtesy of being the daughter of an English teacher, but through long car rides scored by my father's meticulously organized playlists. In my head, I wrote, shot, and directed movies and projected them from my mind to the rain-speckled screen of the car window I gazed through, lost in my head.

Then, in sixth grade, I got one of the best gifts I've ever received. The bright blue iPod shuffle was well cared for. I carried it through middle school. It burned my pocket through classes that bored me, tried to coax me into listening. In my free time, the earbuds rarely left my ears--volume too loud, blasting music I had so carefully downloaded to iTunes on the old white laptop I shared between my three siblings.

We shared an iPad, too, and I made songs on Garageband, clumsy fingers gradually growing more adept, nimbly placing note by note to create leveled masterpieces. What I created, I was proud of, bewitched by the idea that I could make what had enchanted me for years.

The walls of the house still bounce with blaring bass or sway with soothing melodies--from my father's playlists, or from my own. I don't use Garageband anymore; I've graduated to more complex DAWs and more complicated songs. Without music, the story of me is nonexistent. Without music, the stories I tell wouldn't exist. But the story only starts with music.

I used to spend my weekends in libraries. My mom would take us to the local one, and we'd spend hours picking out books. My haul was always the biggest, the heaviest, and I always finished it the fastest. Speed reader, they called me. I was desperate for stories; I slurped and gulped them down, always hungry for more. And when I got bored--stories I couldn't relate to, out of grasp, not made for me--music reminded me that, beyond all else, I had my imagination.

My imagination, firing off so many ideas I could barely keep track of them, telling me I would never be bored as long as I remembered I, too, could create. I've been writing since I can remember, almost as long as I've loved music. For me, they come hand in hand--music sparking stories, stories sparking music. I've made music for what I've written and written to the music I've made.
I would not be a writer without music.

to make a way out of no way

My father has always been a poet. It's in how he speaks—a certain rhythm.
A certain flow. A certain wisdom, too. Lectures that sound musical.
Tap your hand, you'll find the beat. He's a scientist; he pushes language
to the brink of what it can be, hypothesizes punctuation, experiments
until what needs to be said is said the way it wants to be said.
This is how he story-tells, how he makes sense of the truest truth.
What he thinks, what he's done, where he's been, who he's been.
Here on paper, his unedited, truest self. Boy to man to poet,
making sense of the hand he's been dealt. Of the generations before,
the generations to come. Of himself. My father tells me that we come
from people who made a way out of no way. People stubborn enough
to persevere, through all odds. Gritting teeth through the moments
when even you yourself say this might just be impossible.
The strength it takes to pick yourself up, all body and shadow and bone,
and keep on pushing—I have always found it, tucked neatly
around the corners of my father's words, implicit in their rhythm.

j. c. english

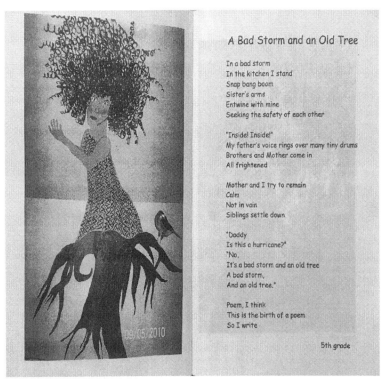

A Bad Storm and an Old Tree

In a bad storm
In the kitchen I stand
Snap bang boom
Sister's arms
Entwine with mine
Seeking the safety of each other

"Inside! Inside!"
My father's voice rings over many tiny drums
Brothers and Mother come in
All frightened

Mother and I try to remain
Calm
Not in vain
Siblings settle down

"Daddy
Is this a hurricane?"
"No,
It's a bad storm and an old tree
A bad storm,
And an old tree."

Poem, I think
This is the birth of a poem
So I write

5th grade

keyramasai english

When Spring
Departs

Written by J.C.
English

to my beloved ancestors, devoted life partner, talented fourth
making us better, and elevated higher ones not yet born
who patiently await— a future shining even greater

drum tongue griotry:
an echoing of ancient beats

drum tongue griotry iv:
middle past griotry

jusfunin'

brothersister

selflections

chance trance

agaperos

drum tongue griotry v:
i om (writing live) still here

lifeliveslove beingherenow

postitsoulstice

lifeliveslove beingalrightnow

cincinature

chi gains lake flowers

drum tongue griotry vi:
of kindred beloved echoing

sankofa soul still sings here

phound phonic phlashback phlashlights

teleportable sublime

word runic tunic

drum tongue griotry iv: middle past griotry

---

jusfunin'

fruiting senses

don't slip on it
especially if your barefoot
it'll be like snot between the toes,
but it goes, great
with honey nut cheerios
or vanilla wafer jello

in the sunlight, it shines
like a crescent gibbous moon,
in a milky cream dessert
it cups fudge and chocolaty syrup
like a spoon,

always in the bathroom,
too soon.

aren'cha
you gonna wash your hands
and get a band—aid?

the hazards of turning juice
into thirst quenching ade.

get that stingy sauce in your finger cut, ouch!
didn't know you were peeling a bottle of alcohol.

shooting out the meaty web flesh
a fountain effervescent, a yellow-orange mess
squirts you on the wrists like a tangy perfume,
sticky face food.

the bitter strong juice
squeezes my inside cheeks
like a giddy summertime grandma.

i chew, best
the sandy sweet flesh
brushing my teeth
until the leathery red skin gathers
into a stringy lump of cud
that pushes back the mouth, like
a trampoline with each chew—

apple eating,
and homemade bubblegum.

9 sep 02

be(at) ugly water

rock
      paper
            scissors

water—

slow down
to win the art of
peace,

to defeat—

ugly   bottles   of water
bend   borne of beauty   to outsmart
weapons,   of war

tool up, what your made up   of,   for—

ripples reefing, more
tranquil shores

1 aug 20

20

story lived wealth

can't googleplex
or make reparation of
yesterday's blank check left,
nor save up the best of today, trying to
add to what we already are and, getting born, get—

living to tell the story of both
(yesterdays and todays)
i.p.o. (s) tomorrows' true inheritance,
with, upmost respect—

our stories,
store, for appreciation
what can be bought in, or
appraised by none—

so, fort knox
and legal tenderize
family circling, to enterprise—

life spiraling
into accumulations
spills out its libations

as currency,
of generations—

1 aug 20

# of an artist unabridged

nothing of sonnets comes from this pen
engulfed by spontaneity i indulge a writer's sin.
writing as i rewrite, rewriting much the same
this freedom must be permissive lest my heart be tamed.

rhyme seems a happenstance -- but a mere coincidence
what to call its happening within the same sentence?
and rhythm is...well, however it goes or flows
those innermost feelings fueled feverishly
by the fervent freeing of my heartfelt happenings.

yes, i am much new at this
though very raw i will not dismiss
although undisciplined i cannot remiss
on my own unique poetic - "ness."

my peculiar rhymes and clashing meters
challenging the dormancy of imaginative readers
my improvised rhythms and abstract diction
shaping new words to cheat evolution.

simile and metaphors make real that most intangible
personified, many other things become humanly perceivable
alliteration of word configuration intensifies soul expression
rhetoric pun and as such question facilitate mind progression.

forging ahead embracing new ideas
and challenges succumbing to inner visions of innovation
a creativity-addiction to soul-felt passion

beating of a true heart and mind
my blood, thoughts loyal not foreign
am i, thou that truest, an artist of abstractions
in the aesthetic poetic.

9 jan 94

sixteen

---

brothersister

unquieted for our sisters

brothers, brothers, brothers...
our silence ignored their soul cries
pride's bloody tears blinded our royal eyes
quieted our manhood on the way through the door
of no return.

they raised our heritage out of the ashes
from oblivion's fate through the middle passage
and sister morisson gave them back to us,
the beloved living-dead.

our asian sisters unraveled the foot-binding
suppression of foot-fetish machismos
and trekked native ancestors across the bering strait,
spreading freedom's fruit across a new world.

when our castrated manhood
ran from the plantation,
died in pride's arms on the reservation,
engulfed the addictive false power
of white lightning's intoxication,

epithets like knuckles of brass
between blows beating into you
our rage's frustration
about a shattered doll house dream
of emancipated manhood's false proclamations;
our coy tantrums of manhood unfulfilled
in northern migration,
and an american dream-inspired
promise land migration,

you my sister,
always...
rose highest,
to the occasion—

held fast to cherished traditions
inspired the spiritual songs of hope that
gathered the scattered weeds of diseased spirits
and planted the seeds of resilient nations,
nurtured an extended family garden.

all the while mourning
a certain death among men,
and swallowing seas of tears
into your undaunted souls' womb
to cultivate cultural preservation
toward our ancient glory's reincarnation.

the souix call it tiyospayu
a warm womb cradling all within,
your inner spiritual cries washing free
what'd become half men,
our halved selves devoid of sistren—

still, you forgave our silence
when they crucified our sacred sexuality
and satisfied libido greed,
raping you, raped me
you loved us back together,
weaving piecemeal remnants of family,

he massaged our genitals into cooperation
we perverted your miracle of life-creation,
abandoned you to the lusting chattel lord
and felled our union into quiet hatred.

drowned our hearts
in adrenaline's thickest saliva
and bloodiest tears,
our open eyes seared
by the sight of festering fetuses
dangling from umbilical nooses,

mothers the strange fruit
hanging from street lights
a conscious-marring brightness
numbing minds into inebriation,
into quietness.

in spite of us
you persevered,
hopeful but realistic
that your proud ancient
warrior would appear,

and yet we were
quieted, so quiet...
quieted by fear—

our sister, my sister
sojourning for truth
in the serpent's den,
held your head high and said
and ain't i a woman?

who exorcised demons feeding altar ids
to overcome his patriarchal privilege—
and rose full bloom from the sati pyre
and voicing sharp resolve
beyond the witches fire,

who proved the fool of us
thinking liberty's quest was in vain
by laying down the tracks
that would hold our freedom train.

my sister, my sister
amid quieted brothers' disdain
weathered and tethered us reckoning
the many scored years, through the pain—

quiet too, brothers
when slick bill tried to ride lani guianiere
to the big house door like a two bit...

when lady jocelyn and anita claimed truth
when sister shirley (chisolm) made a run,
sisters freedom of choice
always under some trigger happy gun—

man made better in quiet time
speaks a silence in helpmates rhyme,
disquieted brothers mark man of right kind
acting and speaking of effeminate mind.

time's long due my brothers
for us to sing
praise our sisters, daughters,
lovers and mothers,

fists unclenched
minds sobered
of resentment's contempt

for aren't sisters all true women
partners in the cycle of life
speaking word to be heard
and spoke, up my dear brothers?

minds
made into faces
mouthing the languages
of an ancient rhythm,

a body the shades
and complexion
of her life-breath.

a nation is not conquered
say the cheyenne,
until the hearts of its women
are on the ground.
then it is done,
no matter how brave its warriors,
nor how strong their weapons—

look around my brothers,
it's coming back again
the struggle never ended
(their on the attack again)
we got to mend to make amends,

their coming to destroy us
their coming back again,
tell me something brother
are you gonna make a stand?

this time
i'll be a man with a plan,
try that shit again
and i'll whoop you ass
all the ways
'til armageddon,

full up on both
good woman
and bettered man—

march a million brothers strong
a billion sisters among us strong,
becoming the stallions of that day
arjuna hillside looked out upon,
singing the trumpets' song—

anything,
for my sisters,
unquieted,
for my sisters.

7 apr 95

a hajji deathbed psalm

the scene is one that crucifies
21 february 1965:

a man lay dying,
his blood dies the death of martyrdom
and his soul spends the remains of its breadth
chiming this vessel like a subtle wind
into echoes and reflections of temporal living,
all is quiet like a vacuum of suffocation
except for whispering...subtle whispers...

el-hajj-malik-el-shabazz
el...hajj...malik...el...shah...bazzz
eh hul...haaazzz...jah...mah...leek...

his spirit now dying flashes back,
for understanding:

little was my name
malcolm, only, would i claim
discarding the chains of slave pains,
a name, lain like a brand upon my ancestors
whose virtue (by slavemasters' lust) were, cruelly, slain
i would have none of that name...called little
that name, became, my claim to shame.

i was...little malcom...malcolm little of
omaha nebraska

when i was him little malcolm
i was smartest in my class
but because i was black unlike you,
you cast stones, called me darky and laughed...

at my dreams, you said too unreal
trying to defer my hope
noose my gift of intellect
by the lynchman's rope.

when i dared still want and think of dreams
my innocent joy fell prey to nightmarish screams,
young eyes fixed on doggish jinn fiends,
gnawing at spirit like jezebel fiends—

judgment through hell fire began that day
my father dismembered on the train tracks, did lay
reaped by the sickle hands chanting lynch mob's creed
that would hang any nigger who dare to think free

my mother, you fondled into despair and decay
tormented her efforts to care
and melted her soul fortitude away,

drowned in an orphan's rage
i vowed to be a devilish sage
in this, i became...took another name
was and became an enraged hate untamed,

a bigger thomas behemoth spewing pestilential wrath
i was detroit red on a fiery hell-bent path.
robbin', druggin', and pimpin' your treasures
i learned to master your evil game being ever more clever,
danced with devils thinkin' god was a foolish gambler
lived the pain of a hopeless life makin' hate the only winner.

that was…until…
the cage came falling down around me,
all too familiar,
a personal hell in humility.

i was thrown into a jail cell
where darkened walls could not hide,
the self-tormenting inferno that destroys from inside,
it was here whence i cursed you for damning me so,
where my cross was unborn and your mercy shown—

powered by an explosion into newfound black pride
a chaos in truth exorcising your blatant whitey lies,
i rose like a lazarus and stared from the cave
thought out a life's work among a people to save,

rose like a lazarus and stared through your eyes
opened my newborn soul's temple, wide
for a black nationalist soldier had become full of pride—

x was my name
my claim to the glory of our unknown african fame;
a panther blackest and agile no leper could tame…
until my own nation as judas would extinguish the flame.

i questioned existence like daniel and job
my faith, although shaken, was all i could hold,
toward mecca i journeyed into sacred space and time
performed ritual promises toward a ka'ba black kiss sublime.

i kiss divine that spelled my enlightenment
your message of truth, through gabriel heaven-scent,
i rose from prayer into bluest eyes staring
looking equally, i beheld your truth
allah u akbar, we are brethren!

it was a gateway into an epiphany of truths
lessons learned…all things material under allah
are many of the one, a holistic lesson
from the most high divine—

cursed and blessed to know wisdom's truth
i bore the cross of job's trials, cursed among friends
stayed the lions, at my spirit's torso, in the den
until this day, when goliath spat back at me
the grim reaper's parade of worldly indemnity.

a hajji revelation
revealed, became, i am
as i lay dying…
el-hajj-malik-el-shabazz

el...hah...haaazzzz...maah...leekkk...kkhh...hhee...huh:

the sky behind our minds rolls forward
and the light of darkness reveals itself
el...eee...eh eh elll...haaaazzzzzz...maaahhhh...maaah

a great book opens
a warm wind turn its pages,
a door opens wide to dying eyes
its soul ghosts cry the cry of birth
like an infant opening to a new life:

allah u akbar it cries
hare krishna, praise almighty jesus
they i-thou-ing bellow in classical arabic chant
as echoes resound like a muezzin trumpeter;
this voicing echoes deeply toward, fades beyond
amharic and babel tongues original
into the hymnals of a garden congregation.

a voice unheard speaks
a flesh with(out) color (limitation) is seen
a name unspoken is known and recited
it says:
"TRANSCEND THIS DOOR
AND YOU ARE NO MORE
MALIK-EL-SHABAZZ IS
TO BE NO MORE."

an enlightened self responds:

"...HAVE CROSSED SANDS OF HELL
ONLY TO BECOME NO MORE
BORE LIFE'S BURNING TRIALS WELL
AND NEED SUFFER HERE NO MORE...

ASCEND TO ONENESS
THROUGH GRACE'S DOOR
FREE FROM HUMAN JUDGMENT,
BONDAGE ON THE BESTIAL FLOOR."

a hand formless, out
an essence, itself true
the part again whole,
temporal with eternal.

countless history black and white
will serve true this divine lesson:

that from beginning to repetitious end
there is but one...and only one,
it is the trial of all humanity
that divine will shall be done.

20 feb 96

31

a sister act to follow

i remember toothpicks
in funny places
you making strange faces
eyes rolled back
never letting me sleep.

i remember us giggling
waiting up all night
for momma
munching animal crackers
a chocolate-less
three musketeers bar
who could save the last bite?

watching you play baseball
seeing clearly still
your red and white uniform
and a hit,
or flag football
you among the best
in rennett park.

taking us home
with phil collins
a sunny day long ago
on u-city's lawn.

sticking up for me that day
you remember
my swollen lip – again
by his hand.
like the elder
sibling
you tortured me
sometimes
and made me strong;

loved me
in your way
making me feel special.

and that you are to me
your own special woman
phenomenally
however, whatever.

always there for me
and us
how proud, you'll never know
loving you big sister
and us forever
no matter...

25 dec 93

32

seventeen

---

selflections

unveiling of a promised land

vendors peddle their putrid and petrified poisons
silently quelling posterity's potentially prosperous and great.
the eyes of battered, tattered souls are charged, glazed
with the bitterness of hopelessness - believing providence
affords them, at best, the most perilous and unenviable fate.

ever-present is this suffocating air of despair and wear
stifling the imaginative spirit,
incarcerating the consciousness of all.

saturated in animosity,
it reeks of the calm before the storm of violence.
and flooded are the gates of this place,
with pestilential showers of ignorance.

a helping-hand is replaced by a jagged knife in the back
the friendliest glance, greeted by most malicious attacks
the childless playground, echoing gunfire's cry
the fatherless child that can only dry its eye
as its mother seeks comfort in the "ultimate" high
and revealed, is the destructive face of ignorance—

this is the ghetto land home i know well
the legacy and inheritance i strive to dispel
for a sense of self i am strongly impelled
to expel from my consciousness all ignorance—

for my eyes once spoke of a malnourished soul
my mind, shackled to the opaque walls of the ghetto.
yet, i have been unveiled and with that - the world to me
the nourishing words of many a text proved most key
to this - my growth and mental liberty—

and i am home
to spread this wonderful contagion
to begin a great plague of
enlightenment.

6 oct 90

a pledge for life

how very restless are the nights since when
the finding of this soul's true content did begin
tangled moments in chaos' arms
echoing within me so bold.
tradition's teacher parts the fragile air
and its fury does unfold,
a character is its goal to manipulate and mold
as a lowly primate's soul it unmercifully scolds.

my soul set free and nostalgic by a sweat oh so cold
yearning to embrace cherished essences of ebony and old
things of which i am punitively and constantly told
such an unfinished soul could neither understand nor uphold.
but though my knees not yet ache with the remnants of burnt coals
doubt not the validity of this ebony & ole soul.

it was the almighty in omega land that quelled my raging fire
cruelly taking the vessel of my soul
yet, leaving my determination's undaunted desire.

to walk this lonely and juxtaposed passageway
cross between the unfettered mandate of those uncompromising,
and yet haunted to pursue, stirred onward to claim
in the name and sake of those we all hold most dear.
envisions of their purpose
black empowerment and scholastic prowess.

stifled in biased eyes who ask for my reprise
though this handicap will surely arise
they put tradition before mine and Its demise
and yonder there lies
our impediment.

in this way i ask will it last
keeping the beautiful Ideals
of which it was cast
or will it defy evolution's law
only for peril?

if it be philosophy, be it of the heart
as my eyes will testify it to be in mine.
for what my body failed to disprove
let my soul's diligence strive to improve
for what is then, truly, the pledge!
never ending - for myself especially.

chaotic moments and blind brotherhood blows,
and the time of its infliction
follow me through life to death's interment
lighting the way brightly
to my potential's prosperity

36

and thus is
the ALPHA of a pledge
to grandiosity
eternally

in the name of the first and of blackness
deprived and yet so steady still It courses
through these veins that is
the essences
of ebony and old.

31 jan 93

d i s d a i n i n g maledictions

the mother tree of life is like all others
its best fruit most dark and beautiful.
we are the children of the everlasting
nurturing rays of this world's life-giving star
alkebulites, know who you are!

darkness - but a metaphorical misnomer, misconstruction
human nature allows one to compare the unknown,
unfathomed to it - and they did.
history preceding pre(his)tory

beyond the grandeur of greeco-roman and byzantine europe
lay carthage, sumaria, phoenicia, beni-ido, dahomey,
songhay,kush, kemet, nubia, namibia,
the dogon, asante, yoruba, wolof, mandigo
nupe, ewe, and the mighty blackamoors.

all the envy and model(ers) of many ancient civilizations.
technological genius, dispellors of "dark ages" - were they.

idolatry for the truly encumbered in darkness
crusading for what were these infidels,
knowledge, cohesion, order?
to lie so much, eternal envy must be culprit
for such blasphemy and concocted maledictions.

like the life giving bee taking
fertile pollen to the next - flower
let us pass the seeds of mental
spiritual liberty to another...brother - sister.
to posterity most pressingly
correcting these blatant historical fallacies.

with the wind or on the wings of "buzzing" articulation
spread the words - 360 degrees - the cycle persists!
fret not mighty alkebulites
your will be-again...
soon

12 jul 92

third eye 'a piercing

i cannot fear the "darkness" for it is others' way not mine
from the fields of the dark world i have reaped the ripest
fruits of enlightenment.
i am newly made knowing truth

this present world order - built by thievery and fallacy
is indebted to the darkness for its brightness,
brick by stolen brick - the thoughts of master masonry
perverted, tainted by the barbarity of the "occulturator."

ours, the third seeing-eye must never go blind.
yes.... we are the descendants of your monstrous
cyclops fathmation, your mythology analogous
to the coy confusion of an ignorant child,
blind to the grandeur it owes existence, restitution
truth be told in the cycle of degrees
Is the destiny of alkebulite indegini.

leafing through most forbidden texts
whose contents embellish my soul
i tend to agree about the darkness
of what was lost to us, but will be found again.

their undying fear of retribution is proof
those among us are not sharing with so called misled radicals
fears most the unknown, undetectable, "invisible" us,
and run these mirroring shadows
toward the wardens of universal justice.

our eyes must forever permeate,
ending the incessance of doubt,
our third i visions providing antidote's immunity
to the alchemic ploys of the tricknologist.

genocidal tendencies?
so haphazard and futile
our mother's best - are we!

color complex is fallacy
consciousness is what we truly be
and speak to the persistence of the cycle
and to ours - an assuredly prescribed destiny.

12 jul 92

the nubian revival

great children of alkebulan
raise your heads from despair
a land of great queens and kingdoms
should you be the proud heir.

while others transcended from
dampened caves towards light
the kings and queendoms of nubia
reached pinnacles of might.

with guns and chains came the intruder
having malevolence in his heart
the goal to enslave for financial gain
while tearing great nubian tribes apart.
on ships of death great peoples were stacked
like cargo that bore no life,
like the menaces they were those "entrepreneurs"
had liitle compassion for their endless strife.

taken a place unknown, far from home
in chains they were forever to dwell
but like the warriors they were, they did endure
leaping free from the gates of hell.

now once again, the time has arisen
to claim what is naturally theirs
because for 400 years
by demand of the oppressor
they have built all that one sees here.

so young nubian warriors
i say rise from your shame
by your ancestors shed blood,
our kingdoms we may reclaim,

look to past triumphs,
to instill pride in the future
or to build new nations of nubia
our foundations,
we must first...
nurture.

a development for life

move in day
and this year's group
makes their way
into a world never seen before
eyes seem worn by
graduation's emotions
charged with anticipation
their expectations
about this world
they've not seen before
reflections
on the summer
adp 1994—

those first few nights,
an ra's biggest fright,
it was a nightmare the worst
damn! i swore i'd been cursed,

yet our patience was rewarded
friendship bonds were started
out of all that chaos.

through a show of hidden talents shared
fears, anxieties, desires about life's direction
you compared, and were ready to explore
new things
summer adp 1994—

hidden study sessions
made up for all those messes
and noisy incidents that had me stressin', out...
i just wanted you to see this blessing
being offered to you
seeing you struggling to learn those lessons
made me proud,

like when you were too loud
and told each other SHHHH!
'cause of quiet hours i smiled at your trying,
applauded your effort for i knew
i wasn't needed any more
you'd gotten the point
of summer adp '94—

late nite
slumber parties
in wayne's back lounge
up watching movies 'til morning...
you didn't see me up watching you

excited about what growth was in store
sometimes i couldn't contain it
not wanting you to blow it
like that night
ya'll rolled to the party
black and white
wanting to fight
for, i mean
demanding what was right—

greg my friend
you called it best
and i hope we're the beginning
of what 30 or so years ago
couldn't have been,
no shame or blame
just understanding and respect
for each other's culture—

it ain't just about grades
or essays,
it's about tackling life's mysteries
it's fears, challenges, frustrations
through preparation
reaching our aspirations
our dream's realization,

understand as you will
maybe not now
but when your called upon
to be in our shoes,
humbled as we are to our cores
about what we're doing this for,
your turn will come too
to give back to you(th)
opening dreaming minds
to the ivory door.

to all of you...
welcome to the time
of your life,
learning from you
i damn well grew too,
looking back my faith
was restored,
through this summer and you
the academic development program
summer 1994—

3 aug 94

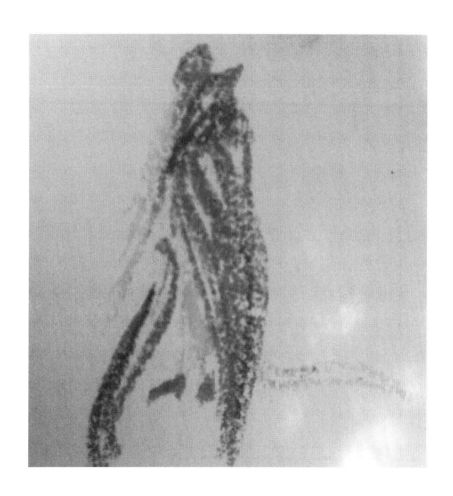

---

eighteen

chance trance

this be a love story divine

i was jammin' on the dancefloor as i always do when that spiritual song of house music
be gettin' the best of my soul and as always some people be cheering me on and others
be mocking my moves improvised moves while still others be pretending they dig this groove
with fake cheers that be the humoring jeers like i be the minstrel show revival and i wondered
in my heart of minds if anyone truly understands yet i be staying true to the groove
that be calling to me and suddenly...about comes this most soulful of soul sistas flexing
her grooviness not unlike mine a frequency so sublime so much the same be ours a vibe train
a train of thinking ours be an essence quintessentially timeless ecstacy matierialized
into groovy moves flavorful flavorful moves that be sayin' things our imperfect humaness
had be grown ashamed to say and so we be talking a tongue universal you know just be groovin'...
bam!bam!bam! she buss a move i be following with one my own i mean we be
the funky funktafied congregation of a rythmical-rooted ritual church that be worshipin' our god

and i be like wow! she really know's what time it be bein' so real she be bein i mean and truest
to the muse of the house groove no frontin' just be feelin' it and don't be caring
about the whispering eyes of persecution and condemnation that be tryin' to crucify
our praise to most high and it be godlikeness that be welling her eyes towards
spiritual tears and have her grabbin' her head shakin' shaken to the mind's root
by baselines baratone and it be His godlikeness of spirit that be overtaking her aura
and be incitin' her seductive gaze infectious that be a telepathy telling tales told
timeless times to the beloved ancestors that be dancin' inside of me and it be
her sensual womanesque moves that be catchin' this soul essence that be the summation
of ancient men and be catchin' my manhood's edenescence like cassius and tyson blow
nuttin' of flesh's fornication or physically physical just subtle friendliest sarcastic soul speech
and i be aroused into sharing my friendliness true 'cause she be so real

and and and when the music stops...and and when the music stops...momentarily...
my intrigue folllows her soul's silhouette and watches cautiously all through the set
that be a cool down interlude vibe of laughter it be the midgroove soulsnack like like after...
it be like the after-intercourse cigarette ...aaaannnnd....i be watchin'

what be her aromatic epervescence of womanhood attentively like the dead dreamer
in a valley of dreamlessness resurrected and awakened by the new day flavory funktafied femme
...i said i be the lazarus born again unblinded by the sight of my kindred the divine-loving child
worshiping through the ritual dance of spiritual song that be house music...in other words
..i be looked and i knew she be different.

so i be laughin' all these jokes with a humor brand new 'cause the jokes be mad phat phunny see
more so because i be seeing how i see things funny more by seeing through her sense of humorous
and the jokes be funniest to the bone 'cause she be findin' them all kinds of funny
and it be my kind of sarcastic slap happy thinking kinda funny and i be liking this kinda laughter
because it be her kinda laughter and i be liking her because she be knee slappin' not to hide her
picturesque smile 'cause she be not caring who be seeing her sloberin' laughter-type a smile
that be laughter most natural like she be reading a MAD magazine on the toilet and be loud kinda
laughin' wanting everbody to hear she be findin' it funny like she be soooh real about how
she be findin' enjoyment in her laughing and i be lovin' her for her realness so
i be kinda chuckle and stop...and...chuckle and stop...and...

stoppin' for a breathed deep sigh kinda funny asking is it real kinda happy...
chuckle and stop-like funny laughing 'cause i be happy in my humor state a state
of happy humorousjoy a humorous sense of sensing things humorous happy-like...
i be that like her...my humor be...
and her thinking funny...much be like me for she be on point i could see
and i be watchin' her smile and i be seeing how she be smiling on my open mind
she be smiling happiness on my mind open and she be on point with my mind's smile
and it be an eerie wonder how we be smiling on point and how we be keeping on point
in the moments that our eyes' sight be on point in the moment that we be of one...

a questioning curiosity stare and it be mad wild i be thinking and i be knowing that i be
found a friendship very special be this friend she be to me and when her eyes be wanderin' about
manuevering through the maze of laughter to find the soul she could feel feeling through hers...
soul that be mine staring on hers she be finding me...and mine be a guised exuberance
within a cheap grin of informality as mine be a cheapened smile a cheap "how you be"
wrapped in a deepest stare though i be meaning to say more but i knowing one be havin' to shrug off
that kinda of realness to save face from showing its trueness naked to desired eyes
'cause you just don't show your "ooh your soooh..." feelings to intimate strangers
that be seemin' casual let alone divulge your selfness to those that be deserved to know it
because that be the dangerous stuff of those asking for the ache of pain to pay visitation
and i be of experience and a veteran of human nature...yet for some reason that be
an unknown why questioning...

you be the refreshing change...a change that be signaling refreshment that be your smile
a refreshment quenching the thirst of longest days in the driest deserts that be misery
that be the arid dryness of misery that be uncertainty and so you i be welcoming you be
you a welcoming sight that be welcoming the coming back the second coming of the muse
as we strattle our selves back onto the spiritual train that be the house muse as we hear
the baseline roar of its engine that be the trumpet calling souls aboard for a ride
into that which be of glimpses toward a reality that be his kindgom...and i be the damned
who dare to be of thinking that ours be of momentary infatuation's inflammation of a hungry
imagination's colorful creation...but lest be told...yes...ours be more so of a true grooviness
truest grooves in trueness a grooves' energy that be drawing us into us...

and we be down for it! we be...we be of communion and so we communed and worshipped
some more in togetherness and though evil be trying to show its ugly face trying to flaunt
its ugly favor by cutting in on or ritual dance glorifying another world...
we be those god chillin' having none of that for we be tasting a mad phat cipher
that be showin' glimpses a glimpse of heaven that be awaitin' those who groove to one
that be an almighty omniscient groove that be incited by the muse of love agape' be the muse
that be havin' us just be groovin' in our haven that be a love of the spiritual song that be
house music a musical house of our philia moving through His door towards agape'-ness...
a glorification ritual of our divine through dance we be...and when the light came to be
it was not ended as my heart that be grateful be heart moving towards a wanting and capturing
of your conversation and your words be of a friendliest dialogue in healing and there be
no pressure nor assumption that would be perverting ours a sophisticated soul sharing
into blasphemy through earthly fornication 'cause we be the bonded soul kindred in love
that be the rawest original good stuff of eden flavoring that be needing no profilactic
combating STDs of the mind as this be an intercourse experience as should be that it be...
it be of our godloving selves...it...it is the IT that be an offspring most fertile it be...
offspring it be...it be a fertile love seedling in platonicism.

yeeeaaaaahhhh!!!...this be a love story telling of a bonding friendship and how it be
coming about i mean agape' like without flesh strings and her goodbye of thankful trueness
not of inuendo sexual but also not of dissing dissidence but more so towards our flirtation's
curiousity that is i must say a most flavorful curiousity like the left over taste on my palate
of something very tasteful that is memorable pleasure to my taste buds that can be revisited
in my mind over and over and over again without it happening again...

ours is a flirting expression of gratefulness and intrigue for it is of meeting you that
i am most grateful and of knowing and learning myself and of you through you and them that i am
most intrigued an intrigue that attracted and can sense the mating ritual call that be your intrigue...
that be our flirtatiousness...it be our goodbye S.O.S signaling the wanting of future encounters
it be our flirtatious goodbye moving us towards our intimate handshaking gesture of the eyes
that bespeaks a more sacred offering of souls and be the oath of our promise to meet here again
to dive into this that be our bond...to be it was to be continued...

for what was soul flint inspiring match sparks became a fire of discourse...see 'cause
the night be young and we be findin' our way back to what be a temporary homestead place
to lay our soulshocked heads and as i washed of me our spiritual excretions
i too showered my soul with a smile of gratitude for having Jesus who brought me into your life
for i knew it must be of Him that she was brought into my presence to be seen
in my newborn mind eye still doubtful that real sista such her likeness still be yet but of mythology...
an eerie wonder how we be smiling on point and how we be keeping on point in the moments
that our eyes' sight be on point in the moment that we be of one...

and yet i found her where?...whence i come out to mingle amongst peoples and i find her where
my soul's prophet sense would see her but amongst them engaged in passionate discourse
it is a discourse and a passionate intercoursing of souls and i am spellbound by her
oratory's deliverance she is the orator very subtlly powerful i mean i just dig her cool realness
that be humble in the way she'll step to you telling you politely to step to yourself
for your own benifit and check how you be thinkin' and i be of excitement renewed
and my pores be sweatin' out my heated aura that be heated by the solar wind
that be her aura lappin' at my soul that be a planet pulled into her gravitationals that be pulling me
into her web i mean this sis be havin' an innocent knowledge about her reeking natural...
a natural passion about her i think not she be seeing...mine be not a lustful perception
but an admiring one seen through god's loving eye mine be...

mine be a humbling perception of god creation...that she be soooooooooh she be dialogueing...
and we be moving into issues prevalent that are issues prevalent and important issues
she be listening to me dialogue about and she be challenging my thinking but understanding
with a sensual sensitivity that be melting the cold calculation that be my logical counter-argument
she be melting me into a compassionate truce of openness that be becoming our cooperation
 of thinking ...for she be melting my position...she be seducing my disposition into tolerance
and acceptance of her way of thinking and i be fusing it with mine as mine
be the melted soupof thoughts welcoming more flavor into its wealth
as challenge be the recipe...she be challenging me...
challenging my thinking she be...

46

she be challenging my thinking but be understanding while challenging me towards my greaterness
and i am loving this woman for her conviction and find my inner ear listening closely to her
and though that i be her senior in life i be him not caring because i be knowing
she speaks like the vessel reborn in god's love and having this known then i know
hers is wisdom fed through his word and then i know then that i am safe in her guard from concern
and so i be watchin' as her trojan horse of a mouth unleashes an army of soul nurturing
into my soul's bosom and her eyes' light sprays the spiritual rain into my spirit
that be flowering good love a trusting agape' for her who be my soul sista divine
and my love grows like a stalk infinite to the heavens when she speaks of loving most high
mine is a towering ascendance into heavens when she speaks of falling in love with Him
that be the sameness that is god i am the felled i be the one falling into god's love with her
and defense be of no necessity or consequence 'cause she loves most high and thus i know
could mean me no harm and her confession becomes our bridge a paid toll into my world
as i confess in her my true self and our vibe grows more intense in understanding and my soul aches
for her tenderness this late night and we need no apology because our loving care be not of flesh
and be not of lusting but of spirit and as the light of new day's intrusion arises and interrupts our
sharing to disperse of us she be knowing...she be knowing knowledge of me beyond
what i had intended to tell her and meant for her to know she be telling me she know
and i then be knowing it is her who be of divinity 'cause she be knowing that as we shared of self
through god it must be 'cause she be a mirror telling me that she saw beyond...

beyond my walls she be a mirror....she be the mirror telling me she be the mirror...
mirror mirror breakin' down walls... she be the mirror bracin' my fall...into her...she be the mirror....
the mirror she be...a mirror telling me...she be the mirror...she be a mirror seeing beyond
my half-truths about self and i am a believer again of she...and of her kind i be ever so faithful
in belief for she be teaching in me more of love's greatness i know working
for his a godlikeness in love teaching me agape' good stuff agape' it is she heard me speak...
and i am a Lazarus under her god enlightened eyes when she calls on me my true greatness
and that is why i am loving her for she for she...for she love's too our as i do
and i am then in safe keeping with her loving of my manhood
her brother who be loving her womaninity...

this be my way that is...of telling
telling you that it was you who affected my world
with our encounter of god love towards a vibe bond most unique
and rarely are my nostalgic mood's journeys into reflection without trips to you and so...
i say this in the only way i know how...no letters sharing thoughts un-guised and unprotected rather
i express the un-expressible directly through the poetic freedom of the muse taking a million words
instead to say what a few might have said...and that is...

i m i s s y o u...friend.
told in this story this it be all told all be told in this a story
it be a story about love agape' love agape' she be
she be said it so knowingly...
this be a love story agape
a love story divine.

for cool j
4 jul 95

heaven's inflatable ark

genesis 1:7

upon arrival
the splash of shallow water (made heavier)
tickling coy giggles awaits those welcomed,
just around an asphalt stone driveway—

a sobering breeze coaxes weariness of mind
to follow a trail of plastic toy rings
and sponged rubber mammals
that lead the way beyond metal gate post,
held ajar by two action figurine centurions—

pink osh b' gosh and yellow geranimal sunday best
blanket a dandelion lawn to complete the path inside,

blink twice, watery eyes
and peel back the hazy disguise
made of pollenated midsummer air
ensouled, animate alive—

noon june sunshine
slaps the glaring mind inside
the parental turned childlike playmate body
kited by our gamey imaginational, exchange—

twining backyard comets
strike the bright yellow plastic
event horizon to an inflata-pool
falling laughter big bangs this homestead cosmos
as, for a moment, happiness in luminosity, bejewels—

baby blue bottoming
below wadable waters
mirrors our play full faces,
like cirrus circling about watery sky

souls traverse
domed firmaments
in the twinkle of playing eyes—

the knocking at my door

my doubt was stolen into faith
by the cunning thievery of unexpectedness,
my mind drowned in the darkness of night
and i was blind to the power within,
blind to an almighty love's light.

you were the subtle tapping on my soul's door
that only my faint spirit's remnant would hear
but the unknown like a bully hurled me,
hurled my excited anticipation into corners
to deprive your entrance
for i was fearful,
i feared the coming of a wrath
that was pain.

yet it was patience
your patient compassion at my door,
your patient companionship was knocking
and it lured my loving instinct into trusting,
becoming a trusting instinct that empowered
my edenescent manhood's bravado towards
a courageous expression of self,
my self, confessed in you.

and though slowly,
no longer was i fearful, as
my fate i began to entrust to us
and with expression i gave through safe medium,

i expressed my real self to you through om,
i expressed my spirit
working in me and we shared in its auric fruit,
we expressed what is our spirit
and found each other, again.

found hymn,
safeguarding our hearts' music
from demonic doomsayer's deafening dancers
trying to lure us into piper's calling of souls...
yet we are souls protected,
souls protected from this sinister muse confusing hearts
for eyed god is protector of faithful hearts
and hippocrene's muse musing to the ears of the caring.

ours is an intercoursing safest
through el of om,
this medium of love,
love is our safe medium
love eyeing, saves mediums,
mediums of safe passage into love,
the safest keeping of one another.

love is the medium,
love is the key unlocking doors,
our doors willingly unlocked,
doors defending souls of love
from messiahs false bringing
love pestilence and pain.

as a love-child i saw you were my sister
and have moved towards you, not away
because i can entrust myself in love
thus know i can entrust myself to your caring,
for i see you with the aid of love's third sight
that is a loving and truthful sight.

i have found a match in your humility
and am humbled that you may exist,
that you are a friend in safe keeping, you are
and that, i will be in you.

welcoming us,
a beginning that is
our journeying into growth
through worship, of our working in love

welcome friend and more to be...
welcome into me,
welcome to my home.

1 jul 95

---

nineteen

agaperos

finding love's truth on memory's lane

much time has now passed
and, yes, i knew we would last.
for we are two of a rare kind
our special love is indeed hard to find.
because of this and other reasons
throughout these many blessed seasons
of others existence my heart and mind
have been too deaf dumb, and incurably blind.
ah! memories of days gone by...

asphalt bedding
water ice melting
adolescence passing
provide audience to
our many affectionate gestures.

sun-ripened, sharpened blades of grass
tickle my hairy legs and ass
as i kiss you,
thinking what the future has
in store
for me and you.

ocean waters beckon and call
smooth, hot sand becomes somewhat raw
as to oil-slicked bodies it begins to claw
us openly daring to have such gall
to do what many saw
as appalling—

pick your flavor little girl
chocolate chip cookie dough
or vanilla fudge swirl
ya' better eat it all
save nothing for the squirrels,
keep the fries for them
and the greedy pigeons too
let's go to penn's landing
just me and you.

don't leave them a tip
pretending you ain't cheap
if you want to be splurgin'
that's a dollar i could keep.

rent one, see one
i don't know what for
either, or, in whichever case
we wind up wanting more.

the phone goes dead
i am alive again
the distance reminds me
why i love you—

the muted mutiny of a captivated soul

in life's most brief moments
time's passage loses place,
our heart's breath resembles suffocation
incited by our body's elation
our inners flowing free
mingle
unfettered by the vessel
propelled by the soul's winds,
we are one—

souls set free intertwine during those love-filled acts
preceding that miracle of life creation.
this thing, experience is most difficult in life
uneasy is its
honest sharing, revealing, giving
to obtain
sustained; only in provoking
the most genuine love's unleashing.

fate has thrown me straight into the jaws,
in the grasp of the temptress, the vipor.
hers is a current leading to oblivion.

yonder looms the sirens song,
captainless i sway
lacking my life-blood
i flood
with stagnated offerings.

port, starboard; neither, nor
though afar, about
lay our signaling star,
calming the waters,
as homeward we steer.

toward us again.
for i have stayed
temptation.
our heavenly endowed
love
always,
my inspiration.

paradisal offerings in love

miniscule in measure is that which incites its presence
infinite are its offerings to the gloriousness of one's soul.
even infinity herself must profess feelings of utmost envy
for at its zenith - this thing knows no comparison.

an intangible nature ameliorates the mystique
of this - a divine cure for diseased and lonely hearts.
kindest fate will afford me that rarist treasure given men,
a genuine eve and an earthly eden - to share.

i'll adore this eve of mine
and the eden-like aura
of
our times
well spent.

her unique fairness as only i will see
that distinctive kiss and touch,
her subtly simple deeds and gestures
all ring loudly of a complex love.

there will be no paradise lost here
not so long as our love will sustain it.
when together our bond will be unbreakable,
immune to the ploys of society's beast.

apart - cupid's sting will linger faintly
challenged by the envy of vice

yet, fate will favor
our love's restitution.

and
none will destroy its flourishing garden
for its love simple too divine,
indeed, prescribed and immortal.

delusions of the spellbound

though i walk within the ranks of the malevolent,
the viperously seductive, predatory
none do i fear, desire, or indulge
for i am content; full of this cosmiclove.

though my flesh should prove most weak
and my eyes, addicted to the vision
of her - the divine's perfect creation

our worst temptation,
it is all fabrication, all an allusion.
remnants of your spell cast long ago.
sorcery of the spellbound.

pricked, stung, entranced by her seductiveness
the fire that embellishes my heart
kindled by your tender soft kiss.
thoughts that embrace my mind,
provoked by her
sacred soul offerings.

so indeed, it is all fallacy
that they shall take me away
as she so often likes to say.

for my temporary admiration
is but a side affect
of the lethal injection
that is her love.

and in the time span equal
to the blink of an eye
is what it takes for me
to simply see,
that there is no
love, beauty, or grace
as magnificent
as thee...

spring 90

56

drum tongue griotry v:
i om (writing live) still here

twenty

---

lifeliveslove beingherenow

59

building seasons

psalms 1:3

today i glimpsed an image
of a man, a carpenter
planing away the flesh of a fresh log of wood
sitting just outside the westtown woodshop
i have never been inside,
(even though i always said i wanted to take his class
once i found the time).

from a distance, i could see
the patient movement of hands
applying right pressure in different places to navigate
ridges and knots and curves on the face
of this imperfection.

slowly, layers of bark gave way
exposing raw inner potential.

a baseball bat? walking stick? An oar?
grandchild's toy? leg among four
to a stool, chair, or private throne?

my first year at westtown
i felt like a felled sapling
being mauled by middle school termites
and grown folks' quakerese words woodpecking
holes in my head with consensus-driven speech.
the grindy sand of catharsis
wore my skin, thin to the bone
and still, you helped me build it,
make it our home.

i'll remember
stonehouse expeditions
to the wagners' farm—
daylight dancing through cowpie pastures
and thomas bean getting one right between the toes
(so he did have sneakers on)

and nighttime walks without words
toward a dew covered hill that seemed to
sit just above a fast moving world, and
put the stars at the reach of midnight eyes,

we proved that three-legged creatures
with five sets of eyes, ears, and lips
spilling words going five different directions,
do exist.

i'll remember, most of all
quiet brandywine voyages
as a first mate
learning to read the water and
the river's edge like reading
the story of a tree in the grain of its wood

how the water is—

where the rocks might mold tides and be shaped by,
or if the stillness over yonder welcomes safe passing
getting' the right oar moving as you quiet the left

pulling water towards you or pushing it outward
stirring it up in circles or just taking your oars
out and letting the current move your vessel
as it will,

sliding down the river,
things seemed to stand still—

sycamores sat along the riverbank
roots clawing to porous, silt cliffs
old picnic tables as neighbors
told the story of a river's seasons
in the highs and lows—

lessons in learning to read
the highs and lows of being,

watching desperate sycamores
clinging to fragile earth while drifting
down the way of winding waters

i will remember
wayward seafarers
a few overturned, once or twice,

coming together and anchoring each others'
vessels travelling from all walks of life,
for a praying silence,

like a reef of spirits
tangled in web of fellowship—

i will always remember
another day, my spirit trying
to navigate a collective past, present, and future
through a fog of uncertainty,

along a way where still waters seem clouded in doubt
and a wall of rocks seem to damn — every passageway.

and i couldn't hollow my unstable self fast
enough to lay down an empty log on the rising waters
to weather the month long tide.
so i dug my sapling roots into
the muddy soup along the river shore,
and waited, and waded,
and wade, still.

flinching my toes from time to time
just to make sure i am still where i am—

feet square
to the ground.

a thriving tree, within
a seafaring reef of others,

a tree flourishing
along the banks of an
ancient river.

5 may 04

phoenix son flowering

*"walking in rhythm
movin' in sound
hummin' to the music
trying to move on..."*   *"walking in rhythm" by donald byrd & the blackbyrds*

his tendriling legs
compel a flowering warmth,

fingering hands lap
at dusty floorboards, like
baby blue flames, crawling
across ashy beds
of kindling.

eyes glow impulse hot,
like pollinating stamens
glazed with the rem[em]nants
of forebearing souls dandelion'd
to the wind.

craning neck and blossom
gain equilibrium,
arms scale the flaming ether,
pedal the charred air,
surrounding, all.

sala son flower,
our kindred rising, tower
to lighthouse past lives'
wishful stalking hours, tall.

*"...i'm walking in rhythm
singin' my song
thinkin' about my baby
tryin' to get home"*

2 toddler corduroy feet
flint footfalls towards footsteps,
cocoon-free firefly wings ablaze
with soular memory in each first step,

images of momma jene's last ones,
salajan soul strolling, begets
love flowers of resurrection
name given manifests
(soul) station, in every impression,

our trek king rajah son, reflects
25 scored generations
walking within rhythm.

roots made flowering branches
traverse first the stumbling dances
of inherited old souls aflame, and
come forth home again—

> *"it's been so long since i seen her*
> *i'm tired and so all alone*
> *i've traveled so very far*
> *i've got to get back home*
> *got to get back home…"*

  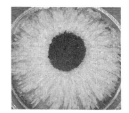

my eyes hajj, his
fortuning us kinfolk, harmonic
beaconing life circular, epiphanic.

he be fire flower walking we,
lazarus magi founding me.
dandelion eye zen, phoenix
son flowering.

his spring, flowers
to mind reminders come alive,
of namesake child he, prophesied
and my soul portion's settlement, momma cried
by his phoenixing, fireside.

alongside, my soul following consigns
his coy babbling movement, us
stepping timeless divine—

28 feb 07

faith understood among spirited hands

galatians 6:9
"...just tryin' to hold on"...   —dying mother to heartbroken son

twelve square begets a certain one forty four,
may our twelve squaring another's, someday
help beget another manifestation, all the more.

spirit gives and spirit receives
and spirit altogether,
brings both into a fuller comprehension.

so much loss
while all the while gaining
these past four years.

years giving questions and bringing answers,
faith calling believers wavering to experience
being, while here now.

far worsening times
den wills' discerning still, doggedly,
the mo' better.

hoping
we haven't spent our lives
mortgaging what had already been ours
to have for free.

male and female he made family,
divine created them exacting worldly fee;
people or things purgatory
about how to be,
genuinely.

and spirit will answer soul querying
with a compulsion to give even more, freely
of who we be; created in likeness—so free.

spirit gives and spirit receives
among first and last (made first) degrees,

and still,
invisible hands—
like footprints valley bound
imprinting sediment sands—
understand,

about pillaring those faithful,
trying to make a stand.

spirit giving and receiving
shares the burden that heavies plow
and ever always has been made
the labyrinth circling
we all traverse,

forever now.
seeds made sapling
flower;
neither roots nor branches
never alone,
even when seeming
deserted to a forest lonesome,
itself.

spirit wills
that
i and thou
be thee.

and am,
evenly
in vice,
able,

to pillar
a covenant ark
that stands,

tiding sea(son)s
of circumstance,

among
open, un-fisted
hands.

2 jun 09

66

life seasons soul

*everybody act accordin' to the season 'dat they born in,
some in the night, some in the mornin', some at noon
some in winter some in june, it's all cool, it's a natural
the science is a jewel, for me and mine's y'allz and yours let's move*   *"history" by mos def*

winter season (approaching) reasons
out summer's excess—
experiences' good and full bloomy,
felled into moody blue grey storms
where indigo memories succumb
to angling deltas of illumination,
refract harvest browning canopies
that shade landscapes earthy hues of regret—

fall leaves, fall
freeing (past life) dendrites
at the follicle.
neuron clouds
empty tearful libations,
monsoon seasons's
reminding sky
to bathe and baptize
earth, recycling.

fall leafy
leaves its bequeathing
for good reasons,
seasoning future seeds' seeding;
leaving life lived legacy
made fluorescent foliage falling,
fallow—at the alter
of its own roots.

balding souls mirror branchy skeletons,
memories dandruff and congeal
into sponging death shawl and exfoliating washcloth
to good feed and good foot
at the root—

fall fells
summertime life
towards winters' seasoning
for good reason,

bare naked branches
wade and traverse their spirited abysmal sky,
as roots earthworm and cocoon
about her placental tundra.

winter season reasons
out of square
in due time circular,
all lain bare.

we trees treeing
see seasons seasoning
for life's reasoning,
out—its (everlasting) truth.

branch our flowering roots'
evolvement,
with soul-sustaining fruits.

springs spawn spells
rivaling fall fells
locking life into wintery dread,
yet spring seasoning smells
fragrant of remembrance
and tells tales told
timeless again and again—

afro leafy & tiedye blossomy
crown these pollinated gossipers
with staccato birdsong remembering when,
spring greening seasons rasta cloudy horizons
that tam tam past lives' live celebration,

spring sprung
images our kingdom come
as plumaged, reincarnating talismans.

mommas poppas, uncles & aunts
grandpeeps cousins, long lost ancients
seed the seasoning,
of us yet sprung,

pollinating
souls not yet flung,
four seasons
sown circular among.

falling winter seasons
never eclipse
an unceasing sun,

summers' seen
never summit
summers' to come.

our most beautiful
seasons
always, not yet
begun—

10 dec 09

us living um in 'em

"tell 'em watcha gonna tell 'em—
tell 'em—tell 'em watcha tole 'em."

a grandfather read legacy in word come alive

when time comes,
tell um.

tell 'em who among um
made 'em—

tell um, i fought a good best fight
so they mightily, might
choose—to take flight
when their inner peace battling
outward armageddons
just ain't felt, no longer, right.

tell um
what we always
have been,
that we took on
the uncertain night
soul battery powering
six, angled upward, flashlights.

and if and when time comes
to die 'specially mine of it,
tell 'em why still try,
how we do—

'bout reaching self- defined heights
and keeping emerging each others',
confounding, in sight.
tell 'em and ask um,

reminding um among 'em
how we brung 'em; of um,
towards times that could would come
when mine (and yours) do be done,

remind 'em; of um,
that it's in 'em,
one sun each; and among.

tell 'em
our lives sung,
sometimes counterpointing
all minds syncopating
discordant still, in rhythm.

all ways,
in appreciation
as living celebration
about the preparation
of the coming—

tell 'em
to well um,
up.

as time, too, will come—

when's my do, due,
if all's already won?

tell um among us, them
daddy made a good mean fuss;
and that being among um with 'em
brought 'em his own kingdom,
home made, of souls' rest—

until he him among um of 'em
was called to give another day
worth hell, to test and
season our solstice soul solace.

tell 'em? tell um—
i am, that   we willed be, them, sum
us overcome—

tell my babies
a story of us,
of fighting full body firm
toward fueling flights
of soul within 'em,
we entrust—

how our time comes
to die each day,
and mine (and yours) may…

and how we do—

gonna give good hell, all the way,
that you give hell hell by knighting each day
by given enemies little time for spelling up mortem,
and spending your souls' body betterin' way,
on a little peace of heaven—

tell 'em
to sing um
like we taught 'em,
and all lives out—in 'em.

even,
when that season done,
does come, along
and i am 'em
done gone home,
within.

8 jan 10

70

espousing solidarity

in
what you see
as vice
i am made (we are) able,
to found and build
a love stable.

wondering,
how
i can, understand
being man
of our plans—

don't make my
high yella
hafta
low blow
ya,

her fair
serene
hafta
show ya,
what elektra
can really mean—

to know thyself
is to be thyself
baring, sharing inner
most self
beside thy selves,

derive
true self
and shine
good self,
unshelf
self
among
soul self,

to coin godly,
our good giving
each other
selves', wealth—

while their moodiness
won't wane,
love true'll sustain
beyond love haters insane,
hooked on opiating the vane.

spouses calling out spouses
framed   incompetent
unmask true,
mother hen peckers,   intent

secreting secretaries
clueless fairies,
high on pride
ferry white mommy   lies

claiming to light the world
with half truths necessary
framing ladyship legendary
and fellowship arbitrary,

spending no time
in the library
of fathering husbandry—

remarry
vows that espouse,
together,

help
mating minds
in enmity,
unify

by
espousing
love
is
solidarity.

11 dec 09

keyra god us querying

summer twenty zero three
driving highway home

daddy, where does god live?

eyes circle four planets enthroned within this
golden chariot atop four wheels approaching eighty,
mine traverse from back to front row
and glance the knobbed leather obelisk
between us-(s)he making them-they, from below

our eyes ascend and lock across a line of longitude
just at the plane where neutral
makes eighty an hour
feel like cruise control

driving eyes remind, and gps
southwest bound concrete steps abounding
like a light-speedy rivery cosmos
just beyond the tinted windshield firmament
splotched with remains of unlucky lightening bugs.

into the air-conditioned ether inside
in the direction us six seated sovereigns face and go,
breathes a flaring up of collective soul aglow—

god lives in our hearts.

if god lives in our hearts, then what's in god's heart?

love—

did make neutral
a certain kind of cruise control
driving meandering highways
home.

31 mar 10

jaiyenan god us querying

fall twenty zero six

jaiye's mind eyes compass
our homebound
weather vane roost,
her guttural words hitchhike atop swirling winds
and make whistles of sea shell ears—

where did grandmom jene go?

fall trees listening wave and wail
and paintbrush a comet tail
upon a pumpkin sun, ushering
this waning shine towards horizon,
just as westtown greenwood grass splays
under six sets of soled souls, a
hint southwest of meadow view 972
where every wind that ever was, is
being thrown about and blown through—

grandmom jene is the wind—

she did what she did
how she wanted to, too—

her jamaica funky feeling
breathes all up inside our soul,
and got all up into you—

hall brow raised
head cocked sideways,
stubborn pursed lips
sashaying hips,

grandmom jene
is the wind—
picking fire red afros
soular flare-wide and high,

brushing ebony-domed temples
that their growing minds'
might, will soon mirror sky.

momma jene
is wind—

stoking our inner glow,
ether river
of pure soul flow.

blown
before us,
trailblazing, sail-raising
life-breathing stardust—

74

a mothering mane,
unbraided rudder of winged meteors
that we ever be lights shown,
shores
shining below.

she is
wind—

we breathe,
even   within our
tabernacles   homegrown
however, wherever
we all go.

31 mar 10

sahnny god us querying

spring twenty ten

daddy, see me jump in the water all by myself?

i did, we were there.
no, i mean in the deep end?

we are always—

always wading with you,
from womb to tomb and again
our little reconciling arien,
coming at life head on strong, living it by the horns

holding
our breathe
and abating fear

since the moment you got born, here—

no toeying it ever for you
belly flopped yourself into this watery below
before you turned two,

aqua boy
knows no greater joy
than wading some heavy water high
that trampolines your vibrant soul
in time with the liquid baptism that moves
body to echo you in laughter,

son shining libations—

our water born star
fear cleansing, life rising hopeful,
dream hard and daring,
water jumper,
knowing, always we are—

31 mar 10

76

sala god us querying

spring twenty ten
westtown pool swim lesson:

do you still love me?

you are my beautiful buddy—

mile wide smile paints curved horizon about his face
where twin red giants make up east and west terminus
blush colored dimples warp cheeky space,
just above eyes seasoning.

a momentary
winter solstice of disappointment
succumbs to eyes smiling words
that spring to life our summering son,

gum gummed gators
can't quell our love,
chew with your mouth
not with your hands,
sala's doublemint play
is all on my pants—

always still loving your sensitive
seasoning moody,
always loving
our beautiful buddy—

31 mar 10

we breathing trees

we breathe
all, in and out
sometimes holding ours,
pressure wells
into suffocating explosives
that can hurricane within and without—

thank goodness,
for spring
earth, loosening
flower, blossoming
sky, sun, shining

and trees,
ingesting and expressing,
channel
eternal tides,

taking no sides—

shade balances shine,
twin-headed roots branch together
suckling an earthy fired ether wine,

full up
soul suffusion supped,

truncating spirit draws line
where breath
exhaled and inhaled
shapes the canopy of mine,

love breathes—

a forest of itself
about and through

treeing
mediums that do—

a chosen
direction and pace
enlivens me,
vehicular
and animates you,
in particular,

love breathes
cosmos

just

as we trees
breathing,
do.

                                        8 apr 10

whole love lays holy down

whole love
punches and pinches
itself, to fashion an infinity
of magnetic lovers

charged to observe and belong
celebrate and relate a self
in togetherness,

love as is making love
what love will be, fully
consummating experience
in love.

whole love
launches
rabid wholes halved
towards rabbit holes, carroting
to feel the loving satiation
of becoming
itself again, among one.

being holed, love
trenches
preferring itself, undone.

man being man,
she nor he of them can
cajole submissions that succumb,
into making each more than
half the whole sum of
love already theirs, won—

every gatsby lover
within us dares trust
a baser nick naturally, jordan
driven by lust
still sober civil-mindedness
guides his reasoning,
distrust.

80

love
science,
beguiling
weds art
to artist—

whole
love feeds, fulfilling
like a finger food tea cake
washed down with soul perspiring
at the palm of lovers' hands.

bees marry blossoms
pollinating lovers play possum,
a holy instinct butterflying,
tethers aching bosoms,

sometimes in love,
lovers amidst beloved, hole up
fearing an all-consuming kind will corrupt,
yet love wills lay us all down
to raise itself fullest, ever enough—

13 apr 10

love living boils down

distilling climactic
of the mundane
is love living
boiled down
to a truest domain

14 apr 10

objective gets subduing you

objective
is luxury and privilege
of those
framing rules of engagement
in attempts
to define real (erasing your reel)

being
objective
is reciprocity and marriage
of wholes
relating tools for development
in hopes
of reminding

subjective selves
to deal in what you feel
to heal and congeal
a surer real.

29 apr 10

when tickling laugh

winds tickle.
winds tickle trees.
when winds tickle trees laugh.

when winds tickle
even seas get a giggling rise
sun blown ones,
tickling sands, move dunes
to roll around on
their sides and capsize.
winged winds feathering skies
cajole outbursts of watery eyes.

tickling tickles inside out,
cosmic laughter swirling about—

when (earth breathing)
winds tickle trees laugh (life aloud).

when tickling, laugh
life loving, itself—

29 apr 10

midwife lessons in just station

ain't no sun for prodigal sons,
pregnant with momma dreams seasoning demise,
without soul-swelling rains.

umbilical reins
hypnotize momma boys' minds untied
now unified and multiplied working to live alongside.

tug-o-wars reign
and husband constraint,
family man mothering sons
facing slow-built dilations.

to hard to maintain
soul home sanctity in vain,

cosmic hormones cloud us
and spell forth amniotic emotions
chosen wife midwives
this second coming circumcision,

she reshapes pace
of life breath we breathe,
hands held together,
in rhythm.

testosterone-inspired
estrogen
of her own
soul elixir potions,
set in motion

leading our world
through, too—
each new day's due,

births forth milestone
building home made
throne, ya'lls own.

...but for one
reason

momma reign sets
to enthrone
a new day sun
of two made
more than   one—

30 apr 10

an eaten garden

mangled axles and crumpled steel hood tops
shape toothless grins of rust eaten vehicles way past prime
weeds mimic joy riders carefree without capacity

scattered appliances bear scars
of battling ambition and opportunity,
once factory white enamel for storefront shopping eyes
now discolor a junk field rowhouse backyard awash
in the leperous decay of hard times

where alchemy of industry
comes clean of its machining sheen
causing all creation to reconvene
of what dominion over truly means—

even forgings cycle down
to align with the earthy brown
of the ground breaking down all things
with more cleverer concoctions,
supernaturals, seasoning—

fresh from an own fiery foundry,
momma hands got to scouring
this junkyard surrounding

knees to earth bowing,
she worked that dead metallic land
until sweat of brow
fed a gardening vision

we could see grow
at the touch of our weeding hands
and harvested in the bosom
of our grateful guts,

blown out our fertilizer butts,
her sheen-free recycling is rooted
in the stank of the muck,
mine now, all grown up—

forty by twelve made six
vegetable vehicles
from an ancient garden
vision compelling,

trying times
casting seed known
that some good god get sown—

an edible ark of manna
atop an endless sea of ground,
will harvest plenty—

stormy seasons
abounding—

4 jul 10

twenty one

---

postitsoulstice

covenance

everyone
is most high bride (led)
and walks, one day
as crucified
to bear forth seed
which lives
inside

when happy in now

every when
that's ever been

happens
in

the dao of now—

1 jan 00

love divines

love is
being able to say sorry
without having to say it
and saying it and giving it
and hearing it and receiving it

love is
feelings that hurt, wound, affirm, heal
expressed with and without word or action
those true and yet trued —

love is
morning breath and smiles,
heartfelt truth as lies
always looking beyond the eyes
imperfection shared as ultimate prize,

hugging hate to death
faith reborn in deep breaths —

love is
butterflies
red-faced searing eyes

mournful confusion
soulful elation,
sharing true
all within you

and me,
love is
no mystery

of what
life is,
love story
in being divine

love is
all of us
messy,
together combined —

1 jan oo

when there is you

when i faced my father
for the first time (like)
looking in a mirror,
there was you.

i'd cry for soul sista supernatural
who'd learn the way and want to love me,
and all along i was learning too,
for there was you.

tore my black self inside(s) out
so all could see and feel my pain
but like some guardian angel
who held my tears and ceased the rain
there too, there was you.

almost sold my life
so i could buy somebody's love
and all along, all along
there was you.

am fighting my way to make a place
trying to chase the mirror's face
and always , there still, is you.

constants i've never known
'cause i've always been my own—

yet when i envision someday's home
and smile with peace on all that's grown,
see fruits of all those seeds yet sown
i'm never, will never be, just alone

for always, there is you.

1 mar 96

92

sun walking on

sun walks
beyond and behind us
planting our shadows
as seeds upon the earth

blooming trees
scatter translucent leaves
peopling world

four winds animate
oldest shadows and enliven
minds with stirrings of past days, remembering
that pillars at the periphery of being

pond edge
pebbles pangea anew,
ancient continents and mountainsides,
water weathered
titans turned tiny damning residue

algae
paint these rolling
water rocks
sun-baked roygbiv
hues

life sways
airy remnants
of a breath blown long ago—

walk, bathing,
a sea of sun
a life alive
amidst everyone.

7 nov 03

grand father to raisin'd son

eighty five
shit weighed and pissed stained
he wears his weathered pride
as a shroud, inside

a life questing manhood
listening out loud done him no good

hospital room four white walls
hold his broken black body,
bed like bedpan, for a body
cess pooled in bile   of enmity—

lifetime work making brittle
rubbed bones, thrown
like worn stones, blown
to a pile of damning dignity

black ancient body
stroke eaten, life beaten
soul seeping
hooded walls creeping
like nooses   on the prowl

straight jacket walls
four white walls,
that stall
an inevitable fall—

wife done died
world, done tried
time done dried, up
by the tide

family just hides
no last goodbyes
drowning earned pride
pride-less proud stride
or god done lied?

matters still none
little passed on
life as a bullet
time being gun
and now you're gone,

the othersided inside
man, to be
my good-eyed
sun guide,

grand son plans
for our next stand—

worry weight heavy lain
bled hope stained,
i inherits old pain
lionizing, my grand sunned mane

legacy of living
in the loving son,

life questing icarus
good eye of sun
taking turn willing that
a grand fathering
will be done—

15 jan 99

good times' era after school snack

butter fried pillsbury biscuits, holed
share hot pans with munchkins, rolled
cinnamon sugar bathed and
into that powdering perfect bowl
homemade doughnuts swell, as
spatula tongues drool —

drinking jello sugar
by the handful,
watched water pot ain't
slowing no goals —

skippy covered ant and jelly sandwiches,
finger flavored dip-n-stick sticks,
candied memories of way back when
sweetening up our childhood, innocence —

1 jun 99

96

love dances sky blues

i danced
'til six am drew
close, thinking i do?

every move i moved
was movement made true

and as i moved
i felt the thought,
i love you

now sun rises
and the sky blushes
dawn blue,

a smile like,
your eyes seeing
clear through

you
and me
make life
new

24 mar 99

always pushin' sumthin'

from bullion to heroine
uranium made for atom bombs
global enrons
gotchu hooked on,
when the sun
still shines free—

11 dec 10

turn ground 'round

strange fruit grows little more from trees
these new world days,
but the seeds still fester underground—

so work them hands
move them foots
sweat them brows,

turn that ground and
whirl her womb that feeds around,

crystal balling love,
abound—

5 dec 10

99

seven up'd souls let's go

7 up half can
sweats in one hand,
seesawing metal tab submits
to straddling chubby fingertips of another,
stem-free with a vacuuming clank
on the whispered count of lap seven

a mysterious formulation exhales its geyser
fizzing mineral and throated spittle
meet each other for a kiss
and congeal under plunger of animate lips

aluminum green body
transmutes translucence
out of grey horseshoe mouth
to hydrate another welcoming body
solsticing lap seven of my growth

drinking while breathing
gas fumed fifty mph el cajon boulevard air
tickles my nostrils on the way down in as, carbonation
concocts another mysterious formula fermenting
inside this boy child half man container

translucence takes on color and make
my three foot worth of mocha brown shape
vibrates, at speed limit holding together fueled cells
propelling her powder yellow subura, '81 gl

we, momma driven like a bat outta hell
to the muffler muffled sound of
you could ring my b-e-hh-lll,
ring my bell!

wienerschnitzel corn dogs and half cans on the go
bug-eyed backseat siblings'   bald cornbread covering
to fertilize their blossoming afros

sunny palm tree mining   mind made mellow
driving reminded   long ago san diego
makes for bittersweet cup of smiles

that quenches a deepest thirst, to know
where and who you're coming from, as you go.

                                                    4 aug 10

100

first thirty five

bhagavad gita 34
proverbs 31:10   in husbanding gratitude

35 always seemed like light years away
back in our know-it-all college daze,

turns out first thirty five
tolerates even less jive—

too.   damn.   busy—

honeycombing good spirit
homegrown at her queen bee hive,
will wielding looks and words
sharp like knives—

to nurture working young minds
she green thumbs whole soul
manna out of life's rinds—

gearing up
her own every woman drive
will powering how, now, she'll strive—

this thirty five plus
eyes the prize
cultivating hard-earned
thirty fiver wise—

life's tiding ride
us together, alongside

6 aug 10

101

eyeing mirrored window view from within

we pay for mirrors that distort
in glass houses built to amuse,
their black faced windows
fish bowl and den
and whale womb daniel souls
like lochness leviathans,
grinning and smiling
high and wide distortions

whirl wide carnival and circus
working hocus pocus
caricatures, to showcase,

take notice—

free ticket(s) taken
cost a heftier token
then mere price of admission,
get you took in so to look in— at,
what plastic surgeon mirror show is broken

a glistening shallow surface, yang'd yin—

just then
is when your gamed up   to go in
and smile inside and glass blow
to know and mirror truth   beyond false compositions,

and mirror, mirror wall ball   chi'd zen
you, standing tall, already in—

window undressing
those mourning mirrors   that stress
lies and disguise,

unsheathe your deeper seeker
then un fog and un squeak speak to defeat lies

unmask your destined prize
manifest, when mirrors mirror the mirror
of your own tries' surprise,
imagine retort trumping distorted ones, will thrive

be good and kind to yourself
respect, reflect, and rise and rise and rise—

25 dec 15

102

thank u teddy g for unsteady readying me

commencement two ten:

still rising right on;
in, accordance
with a soul sewn song

dear ted,
thank you—

for your generous offering
and for greeting a young, wondrous, and confused traveler
june 18 '82 philly international, and
chicken croqettes with ramen topped hot dogs,

kerosene sun spelling lightning bugs,
counting them to sleep among carolina stars,
cape crabbing off hatteras isle in daylight hours,

thank you

for trying to bring a young brother along
best you knew how,
even though you were real rough sometimes—

i'm a father too now
and understand, even if i still don't agree
one hundred percent

thank you
for taking me on as a charge
when circumstances required a man's presence
enhancing, or trying to build on a
foundation of ability and determination

if you can line the paper you write on,
then you earn the right to have something to say—

and when writing time comes
your purpose, no matter obstacles sure to come,
remains clearly writ on right on—

thank you

for your efforts
which, for better or worse,
have empowered mine
through the years—

9 nov 10

103

black man see a chariot sun coming

black man sea
sunning,
navigating among,
knows stealthy icebergs
welling at the margins—

that, if
this lifetime's
lesson

is

to seize souls' service
through saved seers,
shunning

then don't be surprised
by the outcome—

eyeing thous shadowing
any trying shining one,
is all goodness working out
onliest will be done?

belong, or
be dead and gone—
for everyone?

each willing
will burdens
the soul shouldering
its fair portion, of
an ascending foundation.

effort adding
wrungs,
through evolving
generations.

104

complexions
deepened and enlightened
by rain seasoned sun

where reigning sun,
on occasion,
succumbs—

as oblivions
of old,
become dawn;
day made anew,
a shade indigo hue,

hewn of horizons—

and all ways
weigh
atom eyeing
suns,

whose will among,
as foretold, be
so done.

black man sea
sunning among, shines
shine mirroring from—

unseen margins.

each, keystones willing
that all our victory
be won.

9 nov 10

(u) true sung becomes (us) one

commence;
still rising right on,
in, accordance
with a soul sewn song

each and all,
an amen
akin,
given hymn

key minor majoring,
of your own particular rhythm—

enliven
taking care,
to live as written

key major tuning minor
through all conducting, instruments.

sing life
4 even long,
blue bent strong,
off key wrong,
or hook hooking popular
in the get along throng—

commence
right on,
knowing god made
your song,

for reasoning, out
souls harmony, breathing
truth into being
that belongs.

9 nov 10

beauty i is beholding all

beauty
eyes
the beholder,
growing and evolving,
all kinds of certain ways—

10 nov 10

tablet sure table

do you—
without need
of others smothering
want of how you choose

trying to tattoo
their do dos due
(impersonal imperative)
all up on you doing you,

you are
made able
all ready utility
born usable
movable

tabernacle.

sandsmith
your own table

outward shine
your inner sheen,
like a sappy maple

carve legs sinewy
that stabilize
a mantle tabling
souls that rise

a feast of grace
and love with you
in familiar eyes.

11 nov 10

shoring new horizons

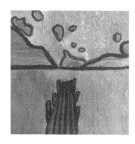

to begin here now
where i am

memory makes
sand and fog
of familiar shores

loving
loved ones
season winded currents
old as days

and set me adrift
to the next anywhere—

another horizon
awaits

questions undulate
while cresting answers
help soul navigate

beginnings begin again—
here, now

16 nov 10

all own one won

do
i-it
see sunned
thou, reflextive

owl
all-ears among
own-heard, perspective

bide
selves, teeming—
potential well, being
ready set
gets to freeing

selfish
jailed fish,
jonahs free
of whaled abyss
ahabs captaining,
mobys instinctive wish—

found
wandering
to belong,
loses all own,

wins
one won
all along,

until,
still-bide
as insides guide
openness to tides,
soul fins
ruddering ride—

abide,
all strides
toward a rise
shining each
in all eyes

prize,
will still
moving—

work a life
all good, proving
made a share
among,
well done, doing—

2 dec 10

auto bio sixography

being jah still
times six degrees
guarantees
momma'll rest
in power and peace—

9 nov 10

is justice

"what it is...
you know 'dey know ...
what it is...
we know ya'll know...
what it is...
you'nt know...here it is!"   auditorium by mos def

just
because
you don't know

what is this is

doesn't mean
that it isn't—

what is it is
to be—

of just cause.

is we are, is
soul manna of stars

made sulfur, ash
breathing gold dust;
is is clothed consciousness.

each is all gives,
a mind building divine, business.

causal is begets, its
multivalent magnanimousness
for all-good is, of purpose.

all is among,
diviners sunning
justice.   5 nov 10

twenty two

lifeliveslove beingalrightnow

will clears clouds

coming from
the only place
it can—

but'll come, from
every (where, one) else,
beforehand

until then
we stand
by our plan
even
when…

i speak
with you
knowing others
hear this two by—
striding, too

so
i say once,
we do—
out loud

will manifest clear
beyond uncertain clouds
love outshines fear,
above circling
fogs of doubt

choice
in action
allows
less talk
and more being
about—

13 dec 10

sol enticing climax

a southbound soul
straddles mercury horizon
delineating heaven from earth,

landscapes grow colder
releasing summer laughter
to fall winds tickling
and winter's vacuuming thievery,

last of earth toned rainbows
bleed upward, vibrant pastels gathering
just below a kneeling sun,
like a bouquet signaling a courtship pledge

longing eyes warm bodies,
stiffening towards hibernation,
that breathe a mirroring incense —

a smoke signal, offering
jealous consent
and sensual applause,

seasons abiding laws
of attraction
death woos life
to cause all passions

their friction
in action
becomes rainbows,
of orgasmic, satisfaction

at descending
solstice, climactic.

14 dec 10

is forces

conformity
is a force

uniformity
is a force

gossip and rumor
in community
is a force

performativity
—of individual truth
expressed as god intended
to be, among others—
is a force

courage to marry
the best of both altogether
and live out full lessons
is a greater force still

silencing silencers
with silence,
is a force of will

20 apr 11

family standing

family
in action
comes, beyond birth
is afterglow dance
of a living universe—

family
shines in
each and all eyes,
and makes galactic star
of who we are
that guides insides

family
multiplies
real reality
exponentially

even if others—
brothering,
don't see
us being we
ain't about popularity

family
don't demand
what to stand for,
family
is the future
elevating
from the present
grounding,
floor

bodied mind
of made creator—

housed home
windows glass kindred visions
wiser eyes soul fashion
domestication in daily rhythm,

near sight inside
ain't far seeing outside—

family
we be
is a
certain kind
of love victory

about love
questing love
made live
story

family
is
she and he, them
made created
walking children—

family
is
music
of sun
some of sum
become
one

family
is woven truth
rightly done,

can't be wrong
when family stands
strong,
sangin out
our family song—

20 apr 11

40 plus a

40 plus a
yokes de mule
soul free made rule-tool
to pay the gifted day,
dat broke full share of life
given all what can
work a life that pray—

40 plus a
yokes de mule to
brand dat cosmic earthy play
denominate dominion
as subject to pharaohs pay,   meant

our sun charge
becomes sum surcharge of labor done
while payday earned always turns many from
fair pay already, all rightly won

rationing down
burden, subsidizing fun—

40 a
right way
get a googleplex
pi integral, place standing
come upon one   cent

mules da yoke
offa soul, aching rest
surveys a square circle
with pointed mind
aimed at da chest   near spent

brute skinned occupants
get thee evicted
under authorizing warrant
of this particular 40 and a
affidavit of consent,

legal regal tender accrues
in endeavoring spirit that barters
love as rent for residents' use—

love lease
lets gardening acreage
furnish its own tenement

40 plus a
don't, won't yoke
dis mule
to pay his day,
beyond what all made up
and out to play life's way

40 a
true due pay?
confuses abacuses,
possesses economists,

indentures monopolists,
gets a gatesnbuffet
one way 1st bank of us lotto ticket,
all aboard the choo-choo mulatto muthafuckit...?

strings the handed puppet
three-card montying free markets,
enrages patriots reenacting originalists,
have social purists looking for an exorcist,
struggling to do basic arithmetic,
embarrasses nine fifths of us
point six times,

draws point made of
infinitely pointed lines,
theorem ain't holding that
number's rhyme

a number
too true terrific
and sublime—

40 a
perplexes googleplexes
times their exponential nexus
3.14 percent interest
computing alone, worker drone proneness
can't write no checks or direct deposit
leftward decimal places insufficient see—

miscalculating 40 a
began its default in the day
(compensating slavery
and 54th calvaries)
of calculating calculations—

40 a
soul
by 40 sum
weighs
none

scale
the drum?
time keep rhythm?

forty a, done
muled de tools
to overrule
that free dom
wills, be won—

28 apr 11

god who is making who god is

"what got up so high in a black hen
that he could lay a white egg?"

from their eyes were watching god by zora neale hurston

sala say:

god made us
who made god and
made that who made those
who made them made god and d'res...

a.   god made god
b.   chicken or the egg?
c.   god is u and us...
d.   so i made myself?
e.   didn't we give u dat dna wealth?

jaiye say:

how did i come to be
if you gave me, me?

keyra play
got us asking what
star clan say

sahnny dismays,
say we muscle covered
sunrays

god made creations
displaying
how we pray

sala say—
what's for dinner,
chicken 'wit eggs?

chuckling mouths muezzin
hands hambone legs
flagellant silly cilia
titillating praise

god minds gaze
suns sunning rays

our laughter amens
sala jah of aiden,
his winged prayer wisdom
enlightens.

6 aug 11

36er sis gets fixin'

happy 36th
tag u it!
get your wish list
busy with the quickness

(even blessed as we are
already livinit)
'cause it's your turn
to just live all out, fullest

life we done learned
is true earned—

6 aug 11

selfless loves oneself

selfless loving oneself
        among others
                defies anchoring gravity
                        for the orbital kind

of ports sought—found
                you go find(h)er

enjoy love's levity
                and butterflight

124

broke real good

hold on to that goodness
you do got
good queen and real being
can't be bought

reaching and teaching
them learn us
how we all get taught,
maximize ma'at

broke beats bling
if you got the real thing

4 oct 11

momma's manna gumbo

gumbo mixture
of love for all times
is why so
much was made up in
the roux

momma stewing knew
her age was out of time, so
she spent all the thyme left inside
on that last batch of gumbo

three times thyme
preserves spicy sublime
anytime salty tears, season reminders
of the when,

momma had us diggin' in,
sweatin through a bowl of life's ev'rythin
each day's portion
her fasted share deliver in—

big dipper ladle in,
gumboed manna from on hi—

27 jul 11

homemade daze

sunday brunch
ginger waffles and home fry
flavored cheese eggs
un-bed, slow mo' buttery,
a dozen lazy legs

post meal pot bellies
hibernate beneath oldclothesblankets,
pillows pillow imaginations,
snoring stomachs' stomach digestion,
gestating fun,
made up into flagellations—

family room'd sun dazed
souls cuddle a warmth we cook,
where sleep booger eyes
eye favorite books

midday pajamas,
stained with natural body odors,
perfume cranny and nook
at   home   free
of condescending looks—

tempering.   time.   took—

monday morning 'larm clock punch
school day crunch
steel cut oated, coffee throated
pbj tortilla loaded

backpack'd lunching,
boys' end (back porch) bunching
family   fueling   day—
long hunkering,

midweek mania
expanding crania,
homeschool homework
humbling trivia
backyard baseball
and playful expenditure,

sanitizing, laundry drying
teamsters tabling dinner
ritualizing bedtime sighing
whole hugs praying, shared   full

tucking(all) in for rem recharging
inward winner, dreaming   soul—

friday frees
thor's rasta ease
as weekend sun
smiles inside cheese,

last gasping fight
of spirit's might
at school days' end,
flight home begins

so good-foot kin
can, get it in
movie night zen,
on the mend,

of family tight
and saturdays' delight —

sundays' slowdown
before the go 'round resounds,

housed home sown
us homegrown,

just right —

7 nov 11

128

free dominion man innate

free dom i, will
dominate, manipulate, liberate
some from
what cons cognate
one divining, religion

still, free dom i in i
will's eye eyes on—

this   free free dom
done right relies on,
relating ions made living zion,
creating each and every   real person,

that   free dom
in eye eyes on

free—

fear fired,
eyes do god man
wrong

cosmic dom
cons connoting,
to forge satellites
strong

dom—

manned i pules,
pulling u
at ease,
into disordering disease
king dom
come on lease

god innate   is ate
freedman comes   late
free   dom   man
dominates,   manipulates

freedom,

fire fear
and hire god,
all ready   free
and be—

free domain, still
meant for man
willed be & will.

7 dec 11

129

mother ma'at to ring

mother
ma'at here

ohm at her, ur
conceiving—

us them, here
begetting every when
and where—

got   made the mule,
but not the 40 acres—

give and take both selves
as us plural creators

to liberate labor's, pangs
all   been at,   since most recent big bangs—

turns our turn to hear
into freedom, we too, rang—

1 aug 20

130

po (break wind) oh do u

i open this window
not for me, but u
married first queen
door open numbering two,

made four selves
eating goop
and doing dos,
wiped their stank pooh
before they even know
how to do
they'wn do, true—

bile for miles
mirror smiles, beguiling
our gaga mouths
belch goo goo fouls,

while selfsame
stench,
perfumes

don't get it
confused,
ain't studyinya 'buse
digest y'wn fumes—

already
humble minds,

zurberting—

choose to amuse
nah nah, spittle spittle
you loose,

farts
don't do
nothing
but fertilize
flowering truths,

compost y'wn
hemorrhoidal halitosis—
recycling you,
growing u,

a composted
self, true
all ways
improves

...poo
on u too—
shewt!

7 dec 11

131

egg on pages

last ins
no rotten egg,
coached to float and
kick with one good leg,

learnt to swim
and share the stage,
we all jumped in
and came up engaged,

our river running story,
across tiding pages—

20 jan 12

132

gangrene thumb querying & answering

if you green thumb a man
down to a torso
how he supposed to grow, erect
an appendage
to love you back—

inner jack
your own navel bean
photosynthesize self concept
in due seasoning dreams

stalk
tall, wide
deep and high
roots, branches, dendrites
down and upstream

flower out at
petrifying seams

fee—fi—fo—fum
demon beetles thumbed clean

jack bean stalk &
green thumb your dreams

3 mar 12

133

shout ins

does the sun really
go in the earth—sala

shout. answer. question.

know much more, answer best
everyone learns, loudest
when outward guesses request—

shout out looks,
shout up the find
enthusing musings,
frees up mind—

shout, i am
to be known,
a loud voiceless
whisper,
to claim
own throne—

23 mar 12

134

sirial untitleds

life is
a denominable
ad(j),verbal

when things fall apart,
re solve
love's salve

thought clouds storm
on the horizon,
will the star shine tonight
sunny other ones greet the dawn—

are any sacred seeds belonging?

a soul soiled hand cultivates flower
and position weeds purposefully,
we shall see what farm's in me—

clouds and waves   bring canopy showers
    shading and quenching   thirsty hours,

      thought dust   allergen crusts
        outspoken   causes choking—

enjoy!   meant
giving up or in   to present,
pre sent   moment livened

20 jun 12

us true grew who

growing up
or growing down
love straight up
and turned upside down
weeds and flowers
feeding ground,

stalking clouds
thundering sounds
caterpillar locusts
greens blossom browns,

dragooning sunrays
smile and frown
dearth among hearth
harvests abound,

us true
we grow
from
in sightings
we found—

20 jun 12

all ated

ceded seed
in cue
bated

inner sim
u (done) ate id

woe man i, u
pulpit ate it

stipulated—

in sem innate
stated,
u sim come latex

pro create
fabricates us,
generated—

help or hinder
mated,
love desecrated
or animated,

chosen or fated?

plateful of grateful,
condimentory hateful,
sense of betrayal

altered state
or poncheas pilate—

brute' today
or soul savior?

22 jun 12

first place crowns

who broke
their first place
trophies,
nobody knows

scotch tape,
and love exalts
what other depose

all those supposing
reside where they preside,
in the heart
of the ready-get-goer—

races raced,
and also not,
won't give that already
hard and good got

you are the trophy
rising above the standing floor,
walking proud,
worth crowning for—

27 jul 12

138

sand eyed vice readable

dear reader—

discovery came to me
between asbestos ridden piping
at the decaying boiler room hideaway
below the classroom level floor
of my 1990 teenage
high school, daze—

ellison
big brothered
my sixteen
and has been
keeping my being
now sixbeing'd
alive

surviving
to strive,

thick and through
stormy seasons
ever since—

his incomplete
juneteenth
still being written,

reminds
that life
seasons sea sons,
us perennial june teens

throughout
living one

most of all,
beloved reader, believe

even in vice—
we, all, remain
i'se able

29 nov 12

broke in love yoking

yardmuddy boys
weaponizing garden stakes,
relate the stakes

keyra icabod's
the left lonside of four
parts framing the loom,
her hands harp crimson and gold
string turned obi

jaiye bindles debris
into a beddable rectangle
northwest cornering the first floor
checkerboard castle square
for a night slept tight,

busy bees all a flight
while we lovers, fuel fight

doors, sores break
anything yours, breaks
toilet, chairs, heads shake
toy truck transformer—
self de-capitates

love
phones in
then, breaking
up or down
redials
connection,
to resound projection

love breaks
its best brokers—

pride, hide
balls and walls down
tonguing cheek—around
about that broken leftside crown,

all uprooted upside down
hammer looming, does rebound
lost foundation relation—together

no matter what whether
might change the weather

love well
broke
strengthens yoke,

keeps breaking
to take in
its own—

will, making   it

juneteenth '12

140

ball down

my testicles are broken—sala

yesterday was up
today is down
six year old bodies
go round and round

juneteenth '12

lemon in law

sat. read. drew.
not vegetables
nor animals
spirituals
on task

impression made
before mark
reassure and pressure

home training not a matter
of aptitude or zip code alone
class five minutes to tell

challenged and successful
positioned to experience both
not broken but stretched
while stretching

how can't magna cums
can't write?

lemon law?

juneteenth '12

142

matrix dusting

when i grow up ima build
bumblebee and optimus prime—sala

the matrix was fake, turned to dust
why didn't the primes turn to dust?

dust rock magma
foundry sun glacier cosmos,
black hole supernova hot & cold,

wood charcoal temperature pressure faults plate tectonics
into liquid solid gas kelvin specks petrified sword forks

juneteenth '12

143

one wheel

one wheel two wheel three wheel four wheel
rear wheel front wheel all wheel drive   we'll drive

who fob key locked
from a distance,
and keyless entered
driver's side only?

don't lock out—

transform your one-seater
to seat the six its built for

lock out for a look out
look out for a lock out—

shed blown and broke off shingles
hang nails and split hooves,
make real compart, meant
for new roofs,

secure a new roof—

juneteenth '12

144

rubber band aids

ouch or oucher
hand, handler, handled
stretch, stretcher, stretched
and turned and folded back
and forward in circles
to hold doubly and triply so

or too far towards
scraps of thought
mind body action, reaction

hammurabi plastic
karma reactive elastic

causal entropy
eye for eye elasticity
shock treatment electricity
of better barter currency,
viable voltage electricity

thoughts please spirit, adhere to words
strongest together
to hold and stretch
under pliable plying hands
and bodied minds, and spirits
changed to twine—

expand and reflect utility
reciprocate ability
project or reflect
protract and contract

grip tight or take flight
assimilation agitation creation devastation

ouch the hand
break the band
string tie the ends
make amends
twin manned able
strengthen the connection
between band and hand
towards more balanced action

acrobatic plastic hands
elastic who man
we plan to stand
rubbing together
massaging both hands—

                                        juneteenth '12

on four hours worth a lifetimes' getting wisdom over stood

"allrightnow "—last word id silence exchanged
      between light-yearly distancing mother and son

a handful of word manna
to chew on the cerebellum or pituitary
like the scraped plate offerings
onto mine

still eating speech too like a bird
knowing the son she help made
always been having an appetite,
hearing and speaking an talking
the kissing young darkness with momma
like mostropolous oldthings—

"i knew you were comin...
g'knew if anybody wouldit'be u...
u'dneeditoo to be settled"

otherwise
the silence
grew, evolved
the wiser

slide show slid
compelling eyelids
heavier towards momentary
levity,

newborn sala smiles
remake another may 31
shared one between mother and son

lashes close
in-time and tune
with sliding image
pulling cheeky a prayerfully,
wider smiling trinity—

mother, son,
father unseen

sinewy legs
mind bedded will, as
burly arms leverage
a vertical pair of inherited
calves and thighs

us standing
and walking together
good footed few steps
to practice timing us on,

146

one more time—
laid momma down,
foots still twitching, and toeing
our soul sonic rhyme

her eye welling one tear
my loving kiss took to mine
this mind wine of her,
fueling thoughts of us resigning

to climb
keep climbing on,
climbing on time
with beating hearts' diene design—

"good night, momma
get some rest"
all right now,
will give my life's best

8 jan 13

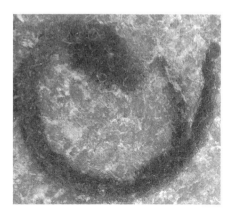

lighthouse comets sail in on

lighthouse pilots
let loose
beyond rock cliff shores
to sea

flickering flames
flint stone armada into combustive titanic,
these waning charges fishschool
and this congealment
becomes phosphoric—phalanx,

maelstrom mariner
in faith, beacons through—
is doubt fog, cutter
of will-steadied mien, moving—
at the rudder.

ballooning souls
breathe in,
and exhale—
each a mast'd lung full
of liquefied hope

underneath and
pushing about—

twinkling obelisk
of comforting aloneness, ashore—
is more distancing
matchstick monolith
ever further—
behind, within before.

its crowning beacon,
descends—
betweens now amorphous
windowing octopi eyes
and continues releasing
a tearful shard of diamond jewelry—

petrifies majestic,
gems, and rapunzels yesterdated beauty
while blushing mind isled ids
lash forward to wade typhoon tears—

of middle passed years—

decor stringing fron horizon
to oceanic floors—
as so many cilia oars,
compassing new shore doors

148

inner vision
captain
inverts and upbraids,
auric nimbi
sirens,
convert and pervade

from sea strait foam
to sky scape dome,
luminal leviathans charred, heavy
in westerly waters
wade nor'easter windwardly home,

where cosmic plankton lactates
and dark matter ladles andromeda stars meandering—
fishnet wormhole looms,

nautical. nebulous. northward

while helmed dreamers
ferry and forge candy striped dreams
into space bridging rockets—

wishing,
fuels comets—

manifest.

good times time—accumulates,
stows away bad ones—

destiny quests.

arrest unrest—
to pile light
and harness, karmic
buoyancy
buoying best,

aesthetic kinetic (beaconing)
pyro midships
at sea

roygbiv hue homing
(pi) lighthoused we
six pointing a seventh toward
all in all, to see

lotusland islanding
lotic anemone,

ransack and hijack—mutiny
(inward) mutiny,
sea sicken
mind crackens
in storming, stability
crows' nest

to request—northstar
indivinity.

memory ports,
possibility, starboard bows

futurity heads —a bearing just set
us onward, sailing—
always   tomorrow,   now

sankofan pow (ur) wow
isle lit, being.

22 nov 13

150

love calls responding

two who knew
two timed three of thee,
out of hard wrought singularity
righteous like easily—

found lost ones
lost worldly,
bound drones
sundered;
done, undered
of love—

these naive neophytes
in love's majestic
did cupid and loop ids
druidic,

aphro-dieted
love buret stupid

so altered—
one on oneness
such t'woed one as this,
dared wander
toward foundation
grounding wonder—meant
to nation on,

to skinner box romance
cornering chaos,

theory
big bang bigger
dualing thalamus, plus

weaponizing,
weeping eye sighing,
storied lore of us—

thus remembering,
ashes memory
into ash-flavored crows
at the pheonixing inner eye brows

that open fisted,
soul combs must dust, and up-brush
to delicense distrust—

to soul food fixes, mustering
a manna of trust
out of unknown's risky
business, justly
naveled in love's lust?

151

fifteen junes worth
of forrest gump't miles,
jenny dreams ginning up jinn discourse
to jinny jobian trials—

yellow bling verity
imaged oz cherub smiles
twining spirituals
cosmogonical. basal. exponential—
battling, cherubic royale

pavlov dogging puppy love,
atuning forks tonality
to life's destined radial
remotely,
channeling redials
of altruistic telemetry,

this time-toned nubile
made self up—to become
one of one—too,
by two, brought two through—
and two more, digitized
this sunning dial

dilated index pointed
out a seventh aegen ward—
dialing heavenward,

earthing denial
speed dialing retrials—
sea shelling
cosmic siren gourd.

each day
lives this faith
initially,

and finally—

always calling.

love
answering
self, reflects—reflexively,
responding,

live life—
corresponding,

in divination—
pondering possibility
and bonding betwixt potentialities—

of polyphonic calls abating
and metronomic (morse) codices, awaiting

3 dec 13

voicing left messages right drumming

responding
i—plural. eyes sing

ring.   ring. ring
three six zero
around—
a full circular rotary,

n—
forking,
atones a tonal
meaning
weighting gravity

g—
of
we,

begat t ing
causally—

in the(e)
beginning,

this get got getting
all going,
our hours tethering
ergots, got got—
effectively,
of me

in voiced fee
and male he be ing,
phoneme—
of telepathy

willing will, i
squares two cubed in
circling pi

wills—lasting
to the end's end tone—
to tell aleph, one
earned true self loves
self all own

chose here   now   see ing
multiverses face epic, known
facing time cellular—i'mmmmmmms'   phone

3 dec 13

spirit u al?

is being doing loving living
among spirit—beyond boxes.

maybe prayer neither—begins nor ends
rather—concentrates souls accumulating and
dissipates and oscillates and congregates,

gravitates and radiates in being—doing love and living
life tried within truth outing and experiencing—all made known

is sentience sojourning to settle, as meant, spirit   home

                                      31 jan 14

an eighth satyr birthdate to remember

lemon butter cake brides a peach pan cobbler groom
at the sunflower patterned alter of a dining room
tabling 8 candles and spongy souls having seen so many moons—
a last saturday (way before last first saturdays of may) bringing sunday june,

an eighth born day with mother sonning love—all in full bloom
black and gold, blue and white tonka trucks light up the birthdating room
bumper car souls fuel life in sirening play—vroom-vroom-vroomzzzzz...

wishful eyes widen full of breath blown like candles
as flickering lashes finger memory weaving happiness—at the loom,

31 may '81 sunshine, surrounding inside and out,
this icing ices sweet as betty crocker—
happy birthday memories confect the heart
of love for son and mother,   forever

31 jan 14

storming calm carries on

supposed to war on mad fronts
while picking battles nobody wants
shut, hurry, speak up
make no mess corrupting corrupt,
squeak this or that due clean
into pipe dreaming forward liens—

give in, out, up giving up
praise enough,
but don't get stuck
in the composting   muck

w t   clk

supple eyes
on prize—

dry good supping
on toughened luck suppers
toughen up,
and dao saliva lubricate
life gruel, rough

metabolize
rough age roughage?

w t   f

digest, in gest
lay waste of all stress,

breathe akindric souls'
own deep breath
dare do will
all this and that   still left,

go on, now
all ways full out—
bereft

strive on, ever
passed a life trial doing—

all to test—

given best gets,
begets shouldering generations
past, and still yet

earned respect—

as timeless on
invests—

due rest

21 feb 14

156

sala signs

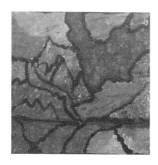

signs mislead
that say one way
when it's really four way
and eight way
counting both ways
@ southbound 202 westtown road
exiting expressway

7 jun 12

bowed arrow spears id

curved stick, harped string
bladed stone propeller feathering

all scales balancing.

treed branches
become trued lines
of boomeranging longitude,

compassing archer arms
eye angled latitudes

shots mark aim,
pointing—
inward gratitude.

28 dec 14

mothersons equinoxing

i'se been a-climbin' on
and life for me ain't been no crystal stair
                                    — langston hughes

"all men were sons once"   —a beloved elder

i am
mindful

of another
spring
springing

falling solstices pass,
laboring last breathes contract
to deliver by her livery—

mothers sonning shine love,
placentas afterglow
an equalizing warmth

another
solstice free being
springs spring,
rejuvenating

other sabbath sun daze
soul full, spiriting

father sons set

atop cement stoop fronting
shoe horn portal at 1402 johnny's way—
about a moving day?

an other
slow saturday elixir
6 may 2006
a certain call to say
who got born you
been delivered away—

this new spring
six passed
10 am again
answering loss
gains us, looses
a life long-bearing
heavy cross

father sons treeing
to take on this
wind-driven moss

sons' sunning
another rising day,
sunflowers
sunning
flowering suns, on
full display
in spectral array

motherson
passengers and drivers
passing and driving
to level scales
womb manned dual stars
at the dimensional well,

this here and there
always calling skyward
every when what where
son-he and moon-she
other worldly appears

last nuptial dances
beyond labyrinth pasture bladed
into totemic ether,
fire circling

on-pedalers, pedaling
pollinate
a plowshare—

saddened gladness, season cilia groundlings
will intoxicate a
gaian pregnant photosphere

gladdening sadness, feather mandible wings
will (sun-mandated) proliferate an
ion nutrient biosphere

granolithic
accelerates and graduates
to scalable fog
to elevate spiritual
above bestial, bog

phosphoric
fragments, ferments
son shine toward midday
solsticing at noon
stratospheric, moon
that wombs
sea sons tiding tune,
exhume diatomic deities
out of marianic tombs—

cosmospheric
sunning and mooning,
chariot souls
in transit
becoming
co-meteoric cocoons,

160

new moon gone darker
krishna universal midnight blue,
mirrors sun come shiny midday shinebow
onward anew,

sadder day satellites
rearranging cosmic lights—
set turning, ignite

sad hearts gladdening
surge and palpitate,
inward holistic

sons' sunning
recharge and reanimate
earthward organic

soular willing sheen
in & out green, some
seasons nurturing, others'
being weaned.

love composts
ore in all, sin

mother son stars
made our sun flowing oars
waning and waxing
candlewick sparks

breath outing, breaths in
a siamese twin

sew we
kin,
can—again
and again—

weed
harvest

moon eyes
begetting
son-eyed currency,
greening over
her fluorescence
underneath,
a boreal luminescence

gets born
an auroric halo
canopy,
sowing
we

so we
can seed,

so concede—

dominion
within
dom in ion

dom in i'se
eyes, on

can breathe
i zen,

i'se'n
her eyes
zion,
horizon—

bordering firmaments
can weed
way, passing age
harvesting remnants

hearts in mind
shine
all day souls,
take hold
their end of bridging holes

alpha beta centurions entwining
give release,
our gamma radiant
delta flares
gaining alignment—

laying down
lying still set standing,
descendent
mudsparks, shoed
in sediment
and robed in soular branches
flora sentient

effervescent evanescence
biota candling eternal essence
condensating frankincense,   fluorescent

settings exchange—
this time, ever
always germinant.

20 mar 12

162

drunken sole at sea in soul

neurons anchor, causing anger
dendrites stretching do frustrate
heartache pistons 93 octane to agitate
mind propelled agents contemplate

bridging thoughts
manifest
across elevated asphalt lanes
of stewing emotions
across wormhole event horizons
bridging memories,

electron accelerant, circling
flint stony thought comets orbiting mind
their exhaustion recycles combustion
stoking foundry mien inside

emotive magma
soulful hot springs
geysers nearly volcanic
steaming dopamine

conscious
boiling kelvin up
to boil down
authentic
being—soupy

epiphany flaming
and medulla melting shower
to reign over heartburn
flowering,

mental condensation
and spiritual precipitation—
distillery of physical coagulation

soul culinary
alchemy
su chef will
in fusion,
cleans indemnity,
enmity, and illusions

envy
tempering
love-mercury,
mercurially sure

simmer
cool
into taller

more drinkable
watery self, allured

buoyant vessel
wading level,
gone deep trench low;
to rue out and roux up marrow—

a cast thought
deeds done beyond
still or waving line and hook
sea mine below,
torpedo missile hovering just above
for those first amphibious
revelations faithful enough
to test gilled wings—

ever takers
given enticing slack
to hook loch ness beastly selves
bellying still another inside
to own flagellant lines of greater thought

fishing out
this acting true
is a catch beyond fish
or lesson, given you

captaining ahab
fishes himself free
of pirahnic leviathans
schooling about me,
drinking and eating and fouling
innermost seeing, i in g be

drink, sail, fish, and fishnet
ole goodness god gave,
each thee at sea

20 mar 12

164

twenty three

---

cincinature

winter seasoning haiku

wind tickled trees   laugh–
even   wintry skeletons,   mime
earth's   swirling   sass

10 feb 15

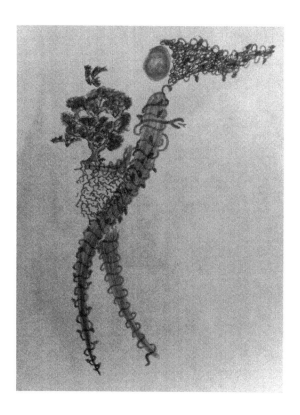

remembering haiku for you

will driven steps, keep
        clouds and rocks out of soul's way
                foots root hymn, they'll (all still) say—

23 oct 15

known words remember

never know
no more words,

especially when the daily grind
grinds into the ground—

take a stay vacation hike
and family bike
where nature, that made you, abounds

trust good training—

that good energy,
feeding good boys and girls' raising,
always prevails

blaze through trying tribulations
forge new trails—
cherish and smile on
what morning walks to school remain,
maintain to sustain
sunshine on, even what rain
might temporarily claim—

purpose fully repurposing wealth
of education, passed on through generations
keep on— inspiring, inspiration

known words remember—

29 may 15

169

live eyes prize on doors

"that the deep heart of nature could pity and be kind..."
from "the prison door" of the scarlet letter by nathaniel hawthorne

near noon september sun
knights a sea of green (swords)
shards newly at a certain attention

mild winds and humming mower
at a distance render hypnotic break beats
that spell emerald mimes wading scorched straw
into doaist waves of karmic dance

none too far away,
eight equidistant pillars
guard a gateway between these medusac (tentacled) sentinels
and asphalt cul-de-sac
where schools ascend from lower to middle
and upper wards

a third coat of fading gray paint
hoods and lays bare asbestos crown
given way to late summer humidity thickening air
and thinning sediments of laboring seasons rusted with wear—
where once upon a dare imagining there, could realize— here,

yet (surrounding) nature pares and spares
along spiraling stairs

here, there
buddy up bushes talk rainbow colors
while companion trees
take on scarlet and orange highlights
that still cannot forestall

eras oncoming
from those that must fall—

wild overgrowth
mirrors receding (painted) line
meant to pillar those trojan walls

as bad hair days and corn row years
upbraid, untether,
blow out comb convention
to signal the good of change within range—

fallen leaves abut
apple core scaffolding left
to honeycombing bees,
whose eager wings siren
what remains of pollen nations—

a colony
of jackhammering workers
and scavenging builders
drum their tugboat sinewy insect legs
at the composting floor

thorax alchemists
make masonry meal of rot and decay
and upchuck threads—
to be woven into a long winter's store

one lone soldier ant
senses the monolith door,
animate cilia gps an imagined—
all what more

as ascendant beanstalks
string ballooning flowers that signal
new shores,

giant eyes fee-fei-fo-fum
an outer space view of ant-eyed vison

here, there, where—

scarlet and white clouds
flower atop and overwhelm
cement foundation that feeds
and holds, like an anchoring fist at the helm

only to bevel, bowl outward
and upward, under the spindle of time
into a more open hand

an oil starved fan
nearby rapturing too succumbs
to storming sirens in the distance
and soup-thick saturation that surrounds

sweat and wind and cloud and rain ensue in time

with the fanning machinery's return,
to ridicule the sublime—

tree branches
armwrestle trash cans
while both straddle a storm drain,
twin obelisk of petrified flowers

being icari—

all tries to vault the power
of any and every hour,
and to sweeten up the now
before it sours

to compost—

what life will bring
and leave

4 sept 15

172

nimbi on canvas

"...we are like children,
we're painted on canvasses"
picking up shades as we go
we start off with gesso
brushed on by people we know
watch your technique as you go..." –painted on canvas by gregory porter

grounded eyes
canvas a kited bird soaring
from beneath and prismatic through
rainbow leafy stained glass that glazes
any gaze beyond the falling canopy of trees

john   henry   elbows
make hammock of mountainous roots
muddy monsoon water—exposed,
these tree toes   are swollen knuckles

hurricane worn bare
by the feathery breath of october winds
that paint sky and landscape
indigo fuchsia pumpkin,
carving cotton ball clouds into
cumuli jack 'o' lanterns

whose nor'easter grey bodies
host but cannot hold
aura and spirit of seasoning sun—

nimbi on canvas
or moon tide windstorms that kelvin
their base charges— gaian seamstress, homespun

these winged nimbi mime capoeira
while yogic earth breathes drum-tongued rhythm
another cosmic canvas
that mirrors and windows, horizon
as landscaped canopy swirls in rainbows, to muezzin—

dazing and meditational eyes
that wonder and wander
about a foresting tree underneath—within,

wind and sun and rain
and decaying earth conspire to conjure

> "step back and admire my view,
> can I use the colors I choose
> do I have some say what you use,
> can I get some greens and some blues"

173

cloud aura lines that pervade within and without
an i-am-bodi made petrified sediment,
of all in all embodiment that weathers its own seasonal imprisonment—

to remember life alive and sponging
a seismic reincarnated soul full   sentience—

> *"we're made of the pigment of paint that is put upon*
> *our stories are told by our hues*
> *step back and admire my view,*
> *can i use the colors i choose*
> *do i have some say what you use,*
> *can i get some greens and some blues...*
> *we're painted on canvasses"*

such that so grounded
a spirit can soar (among fallen supernova leaves, black mole holes,
and dark midwest clay matter)   as black autumn birds   will dare do

14 oct 15

air rowing ides akin

six black byrds
paintbrush stroke upward
left cornering a 60 degree six pm sky,
and fly in turns took as apex
of an amoebic pyramid—

to delta and harness

october wind
pressed toward greater strengthening
and power fullness

by fog bordering
the horizon of becoming
ali baba clouds,

so low
but just above
the batting of their wings
in unison

air rowing ides akin
then syncopation
tam tam polyrhythm,
as cilia walking wind—

their open
beaks tasting air
to map and bear, direction

seem to pucker and drink instead—
airborne fins and tail made vertical,
to rudder and oar
what may lay might lay, ahead—

rivery
school of six
watery souls akin
navigate towards and by
what few remaining buoys

of solar current
help dao way through
october grey nebulae dome
that clouds and reefs

sojourners journeying— home

15 oct 15

stars know dust clouds

clouds cloud
yet comfort and comet
explosions

near and far

night fog vapor
tickles twinkling laughter from stars
that echo cosmic punch lines
lit many light years ago,

day bed pillows doubling as windows
sponge elixir flames
measuring 93 million space miles long,
just solar campfire kindled in the morning dawn,
to fleece over earth's torso
with deep warmth
through frigid winter snows,

those gaseous downy water logs
disclose and enclose—
dam and harness what stars explode
as petrified leafy diatoms below
cover what an axial spooning earth implodes,

this sun shading
cosmos knows, mirrors itself
at polarized nodes—

twining firmaments vow and betroth
pressure and clam within cirrostratus robes,
enrobing the focused mien
of too uv sun and cored earth shine,
chrysalising gorgon beams eyed naked sublime

that fossilize rainbow amoebas—
to image auric mines,

our nearby stellar iris
permeates pupillary placenta powdery pinked
with amniotic atmosphere—

all of us comets
conscript covetous cometeers

and radiate a gravitating gratitude
to satellite and satiate magnetic attitudes,

176

all eyes exchange a batted glance
at natural forces,
french kissing this cosmic meiosis
into and out of stasis

mascara gray cornea line nimbus,
made star lid wind curled cirrus,
make for solarized lashes
that puck and clown a roiling cupid

it is
celestial, terrestrial, and spiritual

rogybiv id made vivid
and good gaia gone, livid—
be within it—

stay puffed marsh magma mellows
make (up) confectionary continents adrift,
islander clouds above these mists
and reefing plates below the abyss,
waltz the angular dance of spinning tectonics

this shaping shapes blue sky lava
into pearls strung near and far—

chakra suns and karmic ones are
all still plosive stars,
boomerang flung rungs among strung
to ladder lasso who you are,

peopled stardust clouds akin
at varying degrees to the horizon—

as a matter
of changing seasons—

earth core and moon orb,
are completing satellites in triangulation—

you eyeing, completes
the square—of composting circulation
and animating, attractions.

15 nov 15

178

---

chi gains lake flowers

seasoning garden senses

a musty mixture
of storm-soaked mulch
and swollen pond is made more bog
by fermented pollen—

this soupy blob extends its algae fingertips
to tickle and lap at riprap dikes abutting pebbled pathways—

diving board branches become rubber band seesaws as
these kited leafy divers flame out incense in feathery descent
and rest prostrated into yellow bricks along granolith walk way
where mortaring footfalls pestle out their remaining frankincense—

pumpkin patch spices
that greet the wandering nostrils
of reid-free wanderers,

emerald green carpeting
and stone statue furniture zigzag
into labyrinth rubix cube
that amaze the plane sight of grateful eyes

sand-flavored stuccos
stem school house walls
nearby stalking trees
teeter over and convalesce

scarred by the sandblast of pollenated windfalls—

these are weathered sentinels
made weary by many stormy adventures
and the similar tomfoolery of charcoal black and compost caffeinated squirrels
who climb, repel, fire pole, and bungy jump with ease

clay tile rooftops parachute the plumage that flowers
a share of this skyward rainbow view
as seemingly 6ft perennials and 20ft titans
take on the vibrant earth tones
of the falling season

applauding winds whistle
as desperate bees buzz
in harmony with the hissing tongue of weed whacker
or gnashing teeth of chainsaw—

all are natural, metronome
most raw

sonic raindrops and musical dew
give this landscape its seasonal moodiness of indigo hues,
all eyes celebrate a toast of soul somber cider
to the tune of a waning star's waxing solar blues,
sonic rain like tonic dew
gathers in condensation atop

pituitary and soular stamens
whose myriad in color
paints a particular falling floral garden—
as an arrangement harvested
by the awe full eyes, beholden

3 oct 16

181

life read in rooms

swollen window sills,
protruding eyes

transport
wintry heavy waters
into the weathered wooden pores
of overcoated skin to bloated doors,

intemperate ball rooms
wallpapered in antiquity and postmodernity
mood swing in mercury,

amoebic and nomadic soul spirits
congregate and exfoliate,
transient   evolving   communing   bodies
learning this lifetime's mystery—

wifi spider webs
ven diagram and waltz
cobbed ones bejeweled by dust,

aged into the chrystal night lights, by moon
that rival gangrene brass ones whose electric compulsion
fools epervescent eyes to feel enlightened by
the gaslight remnants of predecessor days—

black & white portraiture carbon date declarative
past lived moments here in silvery negative,
too, twin flame class roomed subjective(s)
positing of future dreams —imperative

17 mar 17

drum tongue griotry vi:
of kindred beloved echoing

twenty five

sankofa soul still sings here

a brown bag thank you to feed the work we dare do

there is a poem still coming
about us coming together
as teachers and learners

us soul sojourners—

soled rivers converging at a five points' intersectional
berthing of a long long generational—walk,
at the common camp fire of world sharing talk
to phoenix and flint teacher learner shine that feeds
flowers of hope that can willfully stalk
like light homing lifebuoys that map the future's way

(generative) down a well-worn path,
of everyday world changers at the craft—

teaching and learning made exponential
spiritual math—

in the serious made humorous,
small talk inspires
the necessary nerd out
moments of the heart rekindling mien fires—

about who we are
manifest through what and how we do,
branches pollinating at the core
of an all true shared inward driven root—

meeting each other and students
as the world made up to be (in us through us and with us)
as being the necessary glue—

—is the manna
that feeds the need
for you to know me
and me you, too—

global meets local
at the spirited made vocational
to (kin)spire
us keepers kept keeping on
at our little piece of
big work we dare do, in truth—

brown bag soul sustaining (with each other)
to keep supping on (teaching and learning)
with the youth—

7 apr 18

186

(lama) i god in (sensory) sect (movement)

eager and anxious zippers
echo the more muezzin cadence
of creaking doors aged in many such dawns'
concoction of seasoned sunrises
stirred by mile and a half high winds
that turn dew and clouds and the last
of the nighttime ethers, and the early fog
in between, into nature's baptism of a new day—

nightwalker foot steps,
once tam taming insomniac ears,
now footfall foggy daylight wanderers
out of or into dreamy meditation that moves—

miming the rivery movement of ants and insects
divining mirrors of tai chi movement
that windmill breath of life surrounding
to fuel and help mind feed spirit—

begins the prayerful work of the day
that shares   embraces   engages   the momentum

moving about
in the sound and color,

feels one soul   way though   infinite many—

the bristling touch of thorny ground
steeped (in)temperate   smell and taste
of frigid timeless mountain air
made atmoscosmic animate,   moves without haste

dancer   in the amber heat   of the day—

to ignite the sixth sense by weathering
our other earthly five

16 jul 18

lama flagging totem(s)

fourteen t boned fingers
seven each at a hand depart
from half circle triangular cloth sun   set
just below the horizontal
trued and balanced by the up-righted other half
toteming from and above   brush thickening   cascades

plumage of mountains—

this mountainous descent
upon which it rests, is launched
seems to perch or glide—

betweening these feathered mandibles
flags, of pitch night, fiery midday red, and soothing yellows
of just born and dying days, woo the distant eyer—

and the teasing movements
that light winds make, cajole
and peacock this manmade plumage
to ameliorate nature's

and atune the wandering
or meditative eye to see
this kited pinocchio as phoenix a flight—

each finger
angles
a perspective and heading
into mountainous canyon below and beyond

yet also buttresses and balances
the line of sight atop—

surveying in harmony, parallelism, and rhyme
with the far off horizon—

this pillar of our collective spirit,
aloft yet rooted to the earth two miles into the sky—

a collective breath of wind
                    breathes our inhaled one out
                              to remind us to remember—
all spirited beings
                    can still move   with, atop, and above
                                                    mountains
even surrounded
          by a sea
                    of them—

17 jul 18

188

dome entwining domes at the spindle of tabernacled home

well worn paths
meander like webbed bridges
that string the cosmic connection
between tabernacles—

at generation juneteenth

you bring yours
daily here,
where disrobing feet
hieroglyph soul intent in mimed movement
and porch the readied mind and body

to be welcoming, welcomed by
universalist diety

and twin sentinel
gatekeepers,

and a ten spoke wheel
of remembrance,

to an inner octagonal
sanctum—

tile wood floor
seems to glisten under
a coating of its own inner sap
to mirror below
a mirror hovering above   it—

mirroring oblong oval
ceiling gives this it an i, times us,   consciousness—

where sideways and vertical eights
and diamonded framework meet
sun sprayed diamonds of glass

189

to make up
the glory of an eight pointed star
as crown to this orphic edifice—

to ameliorate
the magnified sun sunning
without, within, and at the nexus of in between—

tabernacles entwined make auric   galaxy above
as congregants below share equally powerful
                                       what how thou makes of—

a brought home with each om in
makes this welcome into one—

just in time
to find
way through
an eastern(ed) back door

a screened one making
windowed outside   clay   straw rock
landscaped mirror

adobe alchemy (edification)
building up   inside

sunning wormhole floors
give beneath dome firmament
to a straddling midnight blue star,

dead center of the walled room
when the glass rooftop suns the moon—

out both   (at 90 degrees to each others)
        horizon   (atmospheric and terrestrial)

shows the eyer   believer
all   (that)   is
      within
                              18 jul 18

190

alpaca tao of pooh haiku

buckets wash laundry
    shovel poo, too, turned plant food
        tooling minds could, should, would
            dao did, done real good

                19 jul 18

becoming known

give voice to thought
      and word to voice
          sparking meaning making
               engaging
                    all

17 oct 18

gettin' wise givens song

what starts as sorrow song
stays there not so long, as
dogged will transmutes horizon
bordering right and wrong—

composts it, into self seasoned placebo
made   dared   do   all
becoming of being

that belongs—

every syncopated silence
becoming blue noted utterance
is made capoeira delivereverence
of beloved inner sankofac throng—

soul drumsticks
tam tam(s) vessel holding
carrying   walking   wading on

metronome, muezzins
an ancient song
echoing grateful
(through) generations—

16 nov 18

null god us querying

(peach) basket (milk crate) ball is (baller making lemon rind cobbler out of) life

"rebound 'dat ball
and take yo shot" ut & nell

don't ever—
just
shut up

and dribble

take that (generational)
back handed and boarded pass

to traverse and vault
what's made your fault—

un-evened blacktops
as makeshift portable tabernacles
where mal-nurturing feeders fuel hunger to fast—

soul food as outcast
to outlast—

tube sock practice
jumper game shooting
lack of access
in the trash

worm hole milk crates
from the bottom up, if need be
and iceman finger roll lower school kick balls
so the angels applauding can see
our made mo' betta majesty—

arc it such that this cosmic vibrating orb
never touches the caramelized square
on its way down in and through—

195

show how & what, us
parabolic math magician,
and quantum live physicists,
baller scientists of artistry,
we have always been—

must   need   do

to get us—
gotten through

for us,
we soul striving,
impossible   is   nothing

but net—
willed, do

                        for uncle t

hoop hope's roots in rites of storytelling passed on

balling
is writing is musing
out

your told story
                    in the flick of wrist
as life lived's best hope
        (hoop rooted) of a last shot

                    whether made or not—

                                            15 jan 19

a merry we go willed be

give me your tired
into poor huddled masses—

yearning

to pursue shape, share, build upon
of thee already sung and brought along
to the song we all belong, on—

and create in making up
happiness—

bridging our beloved souls
over troubling seizures
(sea shores) of sadness

over quagmiring inculcations
of yellow brick'd
walled streets of madness—

means
giving already
gotten, as happens—

so happiness,
pursues

each
giving me
to what and how
a unique all getting, becomes us—

giving and getting
self investiture
first

investors sure
shored
at moored shores—
of own birth

tethered
then to the mutual
respect of the bartering
worth of mirth,

held truths
self evidential
made manifest
collective providential

is america—

all ways in the process
of becoming, well coming

quintessential   ly—

comfortably uncomfortable
the place you're in,
is where more perfecting
communion has always been—

so give me love's
resiliency
seasoned of and by
spiraling world story,

yearning

just to be—
america willed,
is love
in all its plurality

willed free,
a merry i go around
we will must, see—

all us bringing ours
makes, thee be—

authentically

1 mar 19

we peopling stars

we the people,
each and all,
are the instruments
and vehicles
becoming and making

america—

not a location
rather relation ship
intersection with
each and all of us so equipped,

taking us to wherever we are
each of us a guiding star
ameliorating america wherever
we stand, sit, kneel, or
lay down as discerning bar—

smallest unit of society
animates magnanimously
in each and all authentic singularity,

drum tongued echoes
of providence,
timeless nomadic transience,
made intersectional transcendence

american made
is made up of global makers

individual shapers,

we are the vehicles and instruments
of making and arriving

taking and giving
wherever each of us, stars

we
each of us—

are
peopling
              soul
are
shining
         cosmos—

are   fifty plus
              furnishing stars

19 mar 19

200

first forty five

kids damn near grown
elders nearly all gone

we sandwiched between,
daring to carry on,
souls and bellies full blown—

hormones hot flashed
mood swings midlife crashed

once puppy lovers,
now matured self knowers,
seasoned co-talkers and doers,

all true known—

hard fought well founded home
out of roots branched to us,
treed bloomy from the compost we've sown
from which four more dreaming
afro minds kited are flown,

we   still   here   growing

towards another season,
almost too soon,
empty nested back on our own
still not and won't be studnya, so go on—

will sugar up some day's grand chil'ren
the minute they get born,
just to be our new day at
and send them on   home—

twenty years later
still not too daily   drawn
to take the time to fawn   on—

on how   long
we been   going
     strong—

'til the end
will keeps keeping us on

our authentic jawn—

19 mar 19

201

app peeling apple tree all wills be

some of these appealers
say don't appeal—

app peal your own peels
roygbiv compost, root, sapling,
blossom, tree, orchard
gaian cloud canopy
of your durable planetary
thought comets expanding cosmos
of understanding,

demanding you stop
counting and asking after others' apples

alone—

apple seed, eco sustain
ably your own,

to reincarnate here after,
cultural cainicide always at you
trying to door-to-door your wokeness
into rip van slumbering docile at breakfast,
soul fast to repast   past
their gmo candied last—suppage

meant to out feed you
feeding yourself
how you do—

fruit of logic won't feel
your appeal,
flowering out of the soul feeding muck
growing beauty from an unwanted bonsai cup,

soil of the real—

app el ohm in hymn
as knowledge of self akin,
a so owned theme,
germinate and incubate
your i and thou dream—

202

—manifestation
beyond deprivation
apple
satiation—

unpeel
worming other kinds,
nurture those that shield your mind,
and feed own soul with home grown edible kind

apple,
an appeal at
a time,

propel
sublime—

appealing thoughts sauce
root, stem, branch, and seed trees
of you and me feeding me—me

recycling mind—

out double teaming society's
pesticide carbonated toxicity

pushing twin bushels
of modified or cannibalized,
as appled in your own eye(d) prize—

composting life as
thrown rinds—

app   led self
realizes—

apple lies

and applies,
a nourishing saucy cider
buttering up the placebo truth,
as freshly fallen fruit
from the inner tree
whose roots are foots
that pillar the soul bridging both

that must needs eat,
bite your own
by daring to be thee

deoxidize,
fueling fruition
of us   we   me, three
treed divinity
meant be

2 apr 19

203

bartering well

impress your self
             own your own wealth

militarize your own stealth
protect your health

buy,   sell,   earn, spend   on sale
being,   already   had & are,   well

bartering   sea shells
at the shore   of your own well—   .

grow morpheus strong
          muscled milked through
                   your own auric egg shell
until this end nells
and next beginning, bells

4 apr 19

ut   n   we   totemic

happy born day unc
just another equally sacred one—

boots tied on until the end
found dating real life lived unstrung
until lost, within
is how one truly alive got found,
gained, and gotten in

slowing down to outrace old soul self in competition
with evolving, accumulating, bettering one   is how to win

a finish line finishing—

to a ticker tape next self timer,
three-fates timing and wading   waiting—
weighing in
on this life's champion,
delivering—

crazy sacred cows
of youth vaulting moons
old-head playing child at heart
soul gone home far too soon,

always missing
and hearing you
in never-ending sun day
conversation at the family loom—

halved thoughts
halved again
as mantling life
have us jumping another
broom   phoenixing—

good footed being
happiness
cracks a michelob mindset
of keeping on
keeping on beyond the gloom

205

as always, all ways—

space i'm in
feels ya'll being, too
in the room,

happy borne day unc
rest in hard won, peace
and we see you soon

us we dog tagged   it
with take cares, outstanding(s) let's hit it(s)—
comes your arien star shine; crooning,

we us spinning
being jah still sextet id,
soul ears and lives
still living it, echoes resounding
beauty   fullness   blooming,
an echo
of your loving

runic tune—

"just
the need
to be
free"

made
manifest
outstanding   reality fantastically

us we,
being
people too,
"too" you
helped   us see

cause
thou n i
dared tell
and   live;   times three

your weight id
in stead of their way
of truth—

until next time
unc—

keep totemic, sublime

we will—

carry on   family in rhythm
and rhyme—

4 apr 19

raising, razing, racing sun in haiku

the sole natural light...
fights its way through this little window"

setting to a raisin in the sun by lorraine hansberry

little windowed light
raises or razes sunned sons
dream(s) rays (race) through generations?

weathered mothers, too
transmute a weary blues, blue
shined to shake woke,   youth

furnaced frustrations
pin hole pin pointing hope's light
beam bars, locking tight

dreams sunned of insight
alarmed out of fantasy
by the razing,   real

sun shine how you   feel
tabernacle soul sized meal
compost, holed stars   heal

and refurnish goals
out shine within to sol soul
beyond redlined doles,

sometimes sitting down
is standing up to make room,
furnish alight home—

raising in this sun
perseveres, as willed so done
shine walls away, sung   flung—

11 apr 19

spiraling life in learning lasso

teacher hands
thread and string and weave
the rope that binds   and tethers
faithful striving as teaching learners   together

buoyed
by diversity
of perspective entwined
and tangled into a   knot

of cognitive tension
and affective dimension

expanding
circled hole, a collection
of chain of being wholes
still pointed   at the spot

vibrating mindful contemplation   in—

thoughts
move hands
at the deliberate event horizon
speed of mindfulness in meditation
reflection in action,

helixing holism
each reach ur   teach or   seeker
lassoing   together
ballooning aura for all kinds of   whether,

each of us
leaning back to inspire
forward momentum
as satellites funneling the magnetism
of a learning axis in pendulum   swing,

wavelength
of light enlightening good will—

enhancing   frequency
teaching and learning, integrity
spirits in their alchemy
it's an age old holistic   story—

hold on
to this letting go   together
held up and tether   ed
by the neuron strings of good

dendritic energy
drawn from within,
bound without,
ground in the shared push and pull
exorcising doubt

give + take question and answering
that ties and detangles   sponging knots
communing, already self-tuning
                    pi eyed   dots,

wholes circling,   themselves
        coagulate   to lasso   ma'at—

amoebic roping belay
spiraling   stir   oar   steer   ur
generative   theme   generator
fuel of authentic   being

what and how educating
manifests   meaning

                                12 apr 19

sundiata epic haiku

words of griot
djeli oracles
griot vessels sung peoples
assuaging quarrels

twelve tribes link stories
eighteen, versed in alchemy
told tales,   sorcery

sixteen four square told
is more chess relatable
check ma'at   able

many named royalty
buffaloed   sovereignty
peopling loyalty

first kings of mali
kindred of mali
sundiata's fellow souls
legacy,   behold!

almighty called jinn
recognize hymn among them
king beyond, brigands

choosing royal reign?
seek fortune and fame?
incubate domain?

initiate hunting
secret arts spiriting life
elevating kings

buffalo woman
hunter prophecies
seven savior son of soul(s)
borne of buffalo

lion child
dark schemes gestate coup
drumming fate owls son coming
birth drum sounds anew

childhood
malice suckles soul
tongued laughs termite treeing soles
gardened love holds whole

lion's awakening
mother's tears fire forge
blacksmith sonning will to stand
iron bowed arrow man

exile
take give leave stay   win
borne akin becoming friends
rage feeds rites silenced

must leave to give back
to yourself what others took
moving stool seats   rook

hospitality
hosts wori worries, storied
questions answer call

war drum drums laughter
bow bender makes people bow
insults stalk man,   tall

djata strides towards
swapping proverbs seizing swords
makes wori of   words

sorcerer king
triple curtain wall
seven story tower falls
nine threed owling, calls

secret griot play
hammer notes, soul sonic rays
room tuned into phase

hurried steps foot rage
seething soul in song suns, rage
kings duel at dotage

history
griots sing story
memory crowns destiny
knighting history

proud tree tempest fells
storm winds at horizon, nells
uproots evil soil

power perverts man
divine magic, salvation
loving, always   wins

abducted love, friends
anger punishing   rivals,
enmity beguiles

calamity questions
resistance wielding answers
mali, sovereign!

old griot sung, sounds
sooth sage magi search around
prophesied,   resounds

sogolon djata!
running   waiting   hunting   home,
mother receive us

why is it ghougou?
mandigo courtesy binds
meaningful glance   shines

baobab leaves
soumaro invades
touman flees fakali's praise
djata mourns, malaise

recognize baobab
nobody becomes somebody
green thumbs sage, mali!

divining merchants
greenhouse vergible mali,
ray manna story

weeping mothers pray
djata saan, find   yhwh
arrow string bow   ray

worded silence rays
manding savior fates' embrace
crowned djata,   amaze!

good night sogolon
trembling voicing wishing son
wells will,   "day has come!"

broken pottery
freeing mother roots goodwill
kings bound word   regal

212

return
husband soul power
midwive gaia dowager
son dark aged hours

snaking evil dies
dragoning phoenix fire flies
king djata will rise

lion mane buffalo
steels iron army aglow
archer   bows arrow

phalanx head tips spear
peoples wishing draws bow near
stringing   messengers

amount treasury
count war won territory
surmount legacy

marching energy
divines relate history
sung, epic story

soumoaro attacks
told story counteracts
outflanks   detachments

djata arjuns valley
soldiers blacken, solars laugh
iron phalanx   staffs

mosaic lightning
thorax djata, frightening
whelms, surprising

totem sword bonsais
lion shepherd, lionized
chiefs prey, jinn joust eyes

fighting valley spate
laughing valley celebrate
dancing news, elate

high horned helmet shines
trumpeting drums voice both sides
courage smoke signals sky

battling returns
hearty hooves kick, dust, cloud sun
sand storm eyes turban

elongate, untangle
amoebic squared rectangles
weaponized, changeable

kneed archers sky quills
elastic arrows rein hills
fell fog sunning will

centering returns
left strike, right stomp, underfoot burns
whistling bowed spear, yearns

sosso sixty nined
sandcastled selves' wind unwinds
melting musing minds—

dismounting questions
answering, tramples hooved earth
chorused song, seeds worth

descending mountains
joy's drum answers warring ones
faith reigns, doubt succumbs

peasent told tall tales
march mema manna, full willed
sounding jihad's trill

unseat surrounding
unsaddle foes confounding
reshape camped, grounding

encircled escapes
darkness overwhelming traps
spinning tops, counter acts

no   great   victory
demoralized unity
griots sing,   story

214

names of heroes
surprising attack
increases sunjata's wrath,
whole rearguard   made half

sosso recovers
sundiata recruits soldiers
son   lights warriors

kamandjan commands
valley, plain, savanna lands,
ally childhood friends—

three niani kings
iron aligning beings
forge   fire for fighting—

avenging uncle
recovering wife,
fakoli baits   strife

djata? trees branch map
root route heading   old mali
homeland blossoms, near

allies meet great plain
kindred savanna called kings
promise,   awaiting

pennants color tribes
with whom begin, end?   describes—
twelve hued onyx   vibe

speared arrows hedge walls
panoramic archery
lens long-speared armies

suns of mali, here
saphohenes singing, there
sosso's troops, beware

gathered tabon cousins
sini   dali   kimbon kin
kingly triad, wins

trumpet drum   tam tams,
brings buffalo woman son—
forged sword,   redemption

all eyeing mali
salute djata's majesty
cure   indignity

drums tam tam griots
thousands throat voiced ancient   do
hymns string bowed arrow

215

nana triban & balla fasseke
sosso unvanquished
bull, ram, cock, slain by hundredth
love, reunited

salutations' rite
situating sacrifice
fugitives advise

triban weeps for joy
remembering frail young boy
now mali's envoy

she never possessed
mother land never once left
never rest in quest

claim what jinn protects
lion-eyed king manifest
wrestling destiny

nobody watched over me
kalla wooed complicity
sistren,   destiny

tabon drums victory
lionizing regal deeds
sung words sing   be free!

sundiata's happy—
sages singing memory
preserve   legacy

blocked river vaults dam
encircled griot chants i ams
cresting words knight (hands) plans

tribal kin shout glee
sword fells great mahogany
souls sheath sol mighty

abiding kings war cry
earth trembling fills sky
moved mountains,   lain wide

216

krina
sorcerers wage war
kings comply, answer why for
right jousts wrong doer

owlish dialogue
weaponizes warring words
most threatening peace?

bravados wrestle
i ams most proverbial
prepare for battle!

swords solve warring mouths?
war chiefs taking full account
faith feasting quells doubt

maghan is mali
sixteen generations seed
tempest-seasoned   tree

strength makes its own law
power allows no enmity—
silk cotton   beauty,

conquering country
make hunters, warriors be
yield mothers, youth happy

wood arrow ireless
put soumaro's reign to rest
through difficult path—

thrown spear tumbles horse
two foot-racing kings give course
djata dodges worst

sosso escapes captures alive
caverned blackness can not hide
wounded, dying pride—

mandingos eye prize
drum tam tams sosso's demise
firefight suns dark skies

sosso city lost
meme prevail without cost
cruel empire razed to dust

217

empire
sosso sons succumbed
when djata marched on diaghan
hurricane sun won—

vainglory, kita
defied encamped sundiata—
war wrestling mansas

mountain pooling jinn
sages sacrifice   softens
assaulting song, wins—

receive submission
inspire great celebration
baptize libation

illumination
star brilliant radiation
transfiguration

found delegations
joined sun djata's bright nation
spring satiation

from ghana due north
sacred mali rooting south,
east (meme) west (fouta) smiling mouth—

happiness warms valley,
suns djata's   authority
united country

kouroukan fougan division of world
to kaba sojourn
hastened huts help people home
still reigns   king robes throne

greetings give greetings
everywhere people gathering
togetherness rings

amen peace   coming
hail   our new sun arising
exalt   savior king

save   human being
love   living as everything
story   joy singing—

drum dance festival
tall tell   testimonial
praise in ritual—

king djata crowns kings
selves' sovereign   free beings
freedom   divising

218

niani
niani gives thanks
good fortune hides misfortune
almost forgotten

griots if then   truth
lived full life stories can soothe—
root minds   treeing   youth

empire pile ruins
deeds spoken long influence,
sing tales   with nuance—

eternal mali
eternal mali
griots sing its mystery
secrets spoke wills   see

eye eternally
sun djiata's   majesty
living   told   story

songhay eyeing shanghai

fair mount 3853
near river west lake
forbidden universes, sol   sacred
sight   scene (see in) city

vortex sees,   seize songhay
pyramid eyes,   bird eye shanghai

ra sized   gaia eyes,
phoenix ashen polarized,
nile   yangtze   schuylkill,
other mercurial heavy wise,
muddy water welling,   weatherized,

eternally,   surmise—

under guise of our witnessing   surprise
so   (outward looking inside out)   visualize

through dynastic cycles
of demise, reprise, and civil eyes   singing   prize

rise, in
recognizing
                                                            23 apr 19

namesake story wishes on stars

not bed time fairies' tale,
four plus generations telling what will
then telling, and telling what was tole— tales

whisperings:

keyra masai maasai MESSIAH
      little   black   headed   leader one
dourajai   YE   jnani yoga   camara
       wait and enjoy this world,   teacher of truth's manifestation
sundji ATA   sankofa   ma'AT
           one who reconciles us
salajan nsorromma   ASHAY   ashay
           winged prayer beaconing good life,   we entrust

whispering at your ears
remember,
for long days
full of life's wars,

who you are
must always remember
came   sankofa,   so   far
in this world of laughing hecklers

for the day will come
when you too must be, bend, stand
that iron bar
already, who you are
comet, your   star!

                             12 may 19

muck wreaths galaxies

"seeing the woman as she was made them remember the envy they had stored
up from other times...i god...most humans didn't love one another nohow, and
this mislove was so strong...she had found a jewel down inside herself and she
had wanted to walk where people could see her and gleam it all around.
but she had been set in the market-place to sell. been set for still-bait. when god had
made the man, he made him out of stuff that sung all the time and glittered all over.
then after that some angels got jealous and chopped him into millions of pieces, but
still he glittered and hummed. so they beat him down to nothing but sparks but each
little spark had a shine and a song. so they covered each one over with mud. and the
lonesomeness in the sparks make them hunt for one another, but the mud is deaf and
dumb. like all the other tumbling mud-balls, janie had tried to show her shine."
                                        their eyes were watching god   zora neale hurston

mud   puddles   galaxy
out of event horizon's   singularity
pi   stirs   muck,   basest entity—

compost and stews, renewing   eternity—

a willingness
to   muck up
in what
all's   made of

is   the only   fee

seed, feed, weed   no need
for other   currency—

forty bucks to mine your own mind
forty buckets of muck to rewind,   replace
these same spaced acres worked overtime,   400 plus years
muling   with minimum, maximum,   or miximum
share of harvest   for souls sapped,   in the grind—

loving muck made to labor in
soul food's   life   feeding swine
mud bath exfoliates the mind   to unbind

muddy up to find   uncouth truth,   fruiting under rinds

grass shines,   seen
atop unseen   watery dirt
landscape picturing minds, go inert
at the sight of sodded shielding,   where pipes burst

manicured morass trumps unkempt roads
where peopling vehicles traverse
what's a wading wanderer in a photo-op   worth?

less about rubble road people traversing
more about quicksand marsh
coated with an astro-superficial turf
icing cake for sightseeing deers, preying coyote johns,
and gamey gators   to golf course

dig quick holes near house and basement's sponging thirst
green gummed gutters over quench a drowning roof about to burst—

holes dug
drains plugged
at curbside view
not nair one photo of,

still,   homesteading   our share of love—

willing hands not above
toiling, toil   at the damned roof above,
to paddy and stake   sod steaks   below
floodable stirred into   irrigatable   flow

meeting at the work   to grow   growth
straight out the mucky ground,
house made home   must   need know—

so   grow—

seed,   weed, feed   landscaping greens   deep
with the stank muck   earthworm nursing
jaded firmaments atop,   from those   underneath—

landscape lifestyle of muckless lives
deifies,   privileging lies,
flowering appearance   of fauna and flora among trees,
all springing from the muck that makes us,   be—

never less than   always more than   us made (i ams)
greater than the muck that makes us,   clay covered   sparks—

compost a muck wading ark
out of the selfsame rotting bark—

growing gardens out of shit
means composting the muckiest   of it
and never fearing   handling what your made with—

every now and then
pristine green needs base brown   turning,
let branches branch their source,   flowers bloom,   what's rooted—

takes muddy thumbs
beyond seasoned   green ones
to   do it
muck, renews it—

watery stardust
beaten down to earthly stank,   ranks
as   most high,   is macro celestial   cosmic
soil   boiled down to,   micro terrestrial   basic

stars   trek   universes
as ugly bottles of ice, dust   fiery comets
to shit themselves into an infantile pile
made newborn   planets—

to season up   muck's main ingredient
cooking up   sentience,   heaven sent,   and
at the heart of   the rue   in
all   life   carbonate—

all   all   mucks up—
so muck whatmuck,   mucks   entrusting it

homer buckets   pleiades, plus—   orion belt
where upturned dark matter   silently,   sups

fueling   universal,   re-ups—

to flower   soul sake,   slow
neurons and dendrites,   too,   to know
clouds   canopies   atmospheres   stars galaxies nebulae,
        aglow
ground   your deepest greens in earthy browns,   to show—

peace   (of mind)
beyond   (bodies at war)
has a   composted   sheath
muck is a spiraling   wreath—

so   make mud pi   with   eternity
ensoul soil   with   solar powered   liquidity—

13 may 19

224

intuit education

privileged   who claim to educate
have the nerve to manipulate   innate   imagination
and call this   education,

while my contribution to lifelong   realization
you'll call manipulation?

your presentation of fact
you'll call   objectivity

my inclusion of inconvenient ones
i represent beyond your aim at erasure,
you'll call   subjectivity?

we educate   educative
to educate self beyond
so-called education (without representation)
and you call that   fabrication?

we say   liberation—

true education, exorcises
free   into   truer connotations
beyond manipulative privileging,
of definers   definition
manipulated by their own   systemic manipulations

teach,   intuition—

15 may 19

225

phound phonic phlashback phlashlights

i'se eyeing god

i'm a
i'se been
i' gonna

let us of i's
my eyes, go see
amongst others and perceive
how we come together at sea
and form into solid shores underneath—

watchin' and lookin' for others' i's
to see us, among thee,
what all eyes be—

i'se be looking at you with my good i
eyes be looking at you with my good eye
eyes be looking at you with my good i
i is be looking at you with my good eye

i'se be lookin' wid ma good god i
i'se eyeing god, good
'cause i'se god good

i, gods
like
their eyes
were watching

24 may 99

228

i have words

i have words
they move inside of me
like a belly dancer spelled by muse

a silence
long abused
i have grown used to
the muzzle of epiphany
shaping words of sound that

name love

for we
as writers
are written through
as we suffer,
so are we used

by the muse

now being one in love,
the words seem few

i know not what
to do

wordless,
word-heavy

a living word
stews

1 jul 02

jazz'd daddydom

ambient jazz
of my life moving fast

three queens (and me)
our dreams, like fuel
baby drool, as
starch is the sheen

for poopy-staining ties and shirts
no linen, silk, or wool
for cotton easy washables
spilling the best of dirt—
like splashed-on baby stools,

too, find
khakis cheating wrinkles
and effortless jeans—
reigning supreme,

as dutiful daddies'
most dependable means—

teach all day, learn all night
babies teething and all
eyes seething, with sleeplessness
at all time's height—

seems unending
ever tending,

yet times move fast
blink and watch it pass,
got to make it last—

comes another season(ing)
of three queens screaming,
making the meaning
of my ambient jazz
a live movement fast,

all a blessed man
could ever ask,
and have—

.

1 jul 02

230

writing a life

i yearn to write like i'm moved
to shape the soul behind her eyes,
yet i must first hear the voice
that might make my works
and move my deeds—

she is not sixteen,
nor is this writing or any
a finished product ever
each word, each day

poet and voice, anxious daddy,
embrace the journey and work in practice—

1 jul 02

reality roux

if the story is too graphic to hear, read, or consider,
then the actual experience   of the teller, liver?

living through experience with storyteller
makes personal and communal, flagellators
drum circling, purning about writer, reader, listener, participant observer
to exorcise and compost struggle into shareable resiliency—

story has always been
narrative alchemy, in reality
it transmutes hate into hope
lassoes the arc of life toward
ohm's harmonic wave lengthy slope—

story as lived, beautiful ugly
struggling, too, to share true
real and wish put action, dared do

elixir of lamentable life roux,
requires you, too
story for real,
is soul armor stew

14 nov 19

spongeable finger mud food one

moonshined nightfog spelled by early am winds nightlights and diffuses
mountainous evergreens incensing insomniac souls

spongeable finger mud food two

organic engagement with
people and place,
your being and all beings
windows sun soul shining
and our sacred face,
let no one corrupt your sacred space

spongeable finger mud food three

walker worker,
be a sponge
wield and work it all
live in one comprehension
called the moment
turned movement, even
if the later moves
towards stillness

spongeable finger mud food four

ret to go
if you don't know
now, will know
you grow

in—

weed is concept about usefulness
can you eat what's here without growing, truthfulness?

spongeable finger mud food five

finding any lost destination
is being it, wherever it's at—

just make sure it's you, grouped together by you,
being grouped with other people

if that destination is an intersection
of others ready and willing to be there,

where here is at,
celebrate
shared ma'at—

absence is presence
i wasn't there but they saw me here
always wherever i be, at
sitting at the door—

sense sentience

the heart and mind smiles
and body moving, eyes glazing over,
and leading other senses,
kisses the world back—

windows and mirrors a cosmic terrestrial

at the crick of
mountain streaming water
galvanized by unobstructed
almost atmospheric rays
of a more intimate mile high mountain sun,
above and inside,
capitalizes the i in thou

shaping   all   one

18 jul 18

238

temporing time

if memory is a good word
for the past
and destiny is a good one
for the future
then what is good for
the present?

        legacy—

                                18 jul 18

be u full

b
be
bea
bea u

t (tea) i (i'd) full

beautiful—

mmmhmm
ohm hymn—

eyes mein

easyning on the eyes

mining mind
mein—

seasoning for and with

soul
suffusing surprise,

sing unburied sing

i am us, we   rising

26 july 18

storm eyed be

storm worn tree
winded puppet at my family

wormwood descending
raining enmity

angels commune in tune
to prune, devilry

hewn from seasoning bark   .
comes (2x2x2) unity

wading like an ark

is storm worn tree
weight will made to buoy family,
at sea
in life's journey

we live community
wading storm of worldly,
to anchor deluge -surviving
being

breathe real true

sum of us is dinosaur pee
and dinosaur poo
some of of us
is me and you
life and death
makes breath of life
real true

stepping upriver

old man and the sea
is in the timeless steps
of old wooden ones,

click click clack

the tuning forked sound
of acquiring learning
to condition the mind and the soul?

knowledge is both
tuning fork and food atop it—

real school, positions
student as teacher, too, who
feeds, herself

what is to be   fed,
self -read, and   led—

9 nov 18

blues ain't no mockery brew

try to   jan brewer   you,
then,   jan brewer you
for not letting them jan brewer you

drunken master maneuver through,   anyway—

1 oct 18

246

esl in ing finds us   transliterating

i'd encourage her to start conversational
exchange words that relate to our senses,
since that is how we fundamentally experience our world
then, move to language of objects,
physical being (person) as well as setting (place)
the body, the furnished room for example
finally to the realm of gesture, motion and action, this moves
the two-way immersion from realm of nouns to include verbs,
from a hug to daily activities of our day

2 oct 18

native alien america

so called last at the finish line
of the american race
might actually have been the first to trace
pathways, foot falling this place

26 sep 18

blue noting singularity

pulsar lone (if must)
as echoing cosmos,
metronomes (harp stringing stardust)

19 feb 19

in compass you

people can be a trip,
and momma used to say
don't   ever,   even—

and so try not to only traverse
the narrow path of our
outward projecting ones,

aim to steer inward trippers
to map and gps your compass
to lock on   your steady heading,
of you doing
and becoming trued,
toward the journey to the horizon
of becoming,   you

19 feb 19

250

jus mantric sayings

if ain't nobody your worsers
then ain't no somebody my betters,

so don't let trees get in your way
of you seeding and treeing you,

shame it took a law for some things,
shame they made a law for other things—

10 may 19

womb yeomen

some men don't know
how to be and own
the men all readied in them,
and some women don't know
how to treat um—

13 sep 18

wish sandwich generating dreams

she on her way
and i'm tryna stay
outta hers   but,   be there

letting go on both ends   is
a mean   generational   sammich

6 sep 18

big inspires outside in made up out?

hangzhou, wuxan cities
built big out,   to inspire   big in

19 jun 18

postcard thank you china trip 2018

greetings doctor: first, i want to reiterate my gratitude for the
opportunity to visit china this past summer. the hospitality was
amazing. what stays with me most are my treks to areas being
among everyday people doing everyday life. the language of it
felt universally translatable.

most epiphanic? leaving a final meal we had walked to in a
neighborhood village that reminded me of "the bottom" that abuts
university city, philadelphia mere miles but really light years from
upenn and drexel. storefronts in mandarin next to those in arabic
wore the wear of universal strivings i grew up around myself.

then, a portrait of an in vice able young man, i knew, emerged in
front of me. i saw his playful silhouette scamper down an alley
way betweening two restaurants. he made futbol of some object
strewn at the makeshift pitch of the ground and imagined a goal
that he targeted and shot—at. arms up, he scored. looked back,
saw me watching and dashed off into some leaning compartment
seemingly, home. right then, through time and space, i realized i
wasn't that far from my own from long ago.

so, honestly. this best expresses my interest and gratitude
surrounding another HOSS opportunity at LFA. this particular lens i
feel and know relates, connects us all in a common struggle
perhaps at least as much if not more than it divides.
respect to you doctor for this part of your ongoing legacy.

5 apr 19

255

all mosting dust

that

is me
of degree
telling he (of them)

take it easy
through this body

is us   made   we
being compost,
temporal   host
incubating   cosmos
fertilizing   holy ghost,

that   and   this
making most,   of dust

6 aug 19

happy 44 more

forty four is the new twenty four
looking forward to twenty more,
even four more score (eighty years)
ain't too much to aim for—

you've earned every threshold at life's door
so much for you and us still, in store
forty plus, rings now, to your authentic core
no longer just know, now be the source—

always remember,
scrambling pancakes at A4—

6 aug 19

twenty seven

---

teleportable sublime

seeing chi in awe

tienanmen square
forbidden city thai lunch
daoist temple of heaven
pearl market   the gate—

we started our day two jaunt
through a misty beijing morning
to visit tienanmen square,
an impressive portrait of chairman mao
welcomed us there, as gatekeeper to the nine gates
of the forbidden city—

we traversed this too with awe
only supplanted or better yet ameliorated
by the awesome splendor of the taoist temple of heaven
feats of mind, collective body, and universal timeless soul no doubt

my people   our people—

we restored and rejuvenated
at very siam thai for lunch
more delicious flavor and variety abounded, again
eclectic decor and soulful smile greeted us, within
beijing's best thai! no doubt—

after lunch, meant
another test of will and patience
through trafficked second ring road to
the pearl market which proved a good prep

for the mandated haggle expected,
to between yeses and noes for great buys
hard to find back home

we closed our last full one in beijing
with a fabulous meal among friends
and chinese opera, magic, dance
as well as shared father's day cake,

good people   chi people—

this is an amazing place
enriched by amazing souls—

17 jun 18

260

eye gods

their eyes were watching god
watching god were their eyes,
watching god were thou and I
thou and i are watching god,

thee and i(s) are watching god
watching god are thee i twin soul bodied,
thou one and i two are watching,   godded
i one and i two are god watching godly them
your eyes are god watching,

seeing makes them (your eyes i goding) plurally
their eyes were watching god equals, i god sentenced simply
glance from god, is
god watching,   god   watching god id

first loved sight, is when i
saw eyes i'd (eyed) been watching
my self with all my life with
through someone else,   is

14 may 19

261

eye stars

eyes do as stars do
thou and eye, i each other
as gravitation balances radiation
starring equilibrium, between implosion and explosion,
to stabilize,   stars

eyes watching each other
glance sunners
at the cosmic dance,
dark matter fuels the universal trance
eyes prance   on
as galaxies colliding, enhance   cosmos

some muck unstucks

sometimes
being in,
you got to go back
to nature's   muck

to escape
society,   stuck
in its own

14 may 19

in questioning answer

the question, is
you already know the answer to
who going to get down in that muck with you?

not just prance around in the flowers
but get down and wade through, muddiest waters
with you   true?

be drum being

beat
drum?
    be at, it

       and   be it—

30 apr 19

266

---

word runic tunic

el of all   ant eyes living cured

"...for a moment, paradise..."
mrs. kendall
from the elephant man by bernard pomerance

john hurt's joseph merrick
circa 1980   had doctor momma nurse
outta the mortar & pestle alchemy   of her own spiritual purse
she womb man upped   home remedy   to life of sickness   & curse

trying to escape mobs, gains bigger ones   attention
couldn't be spared, when you   needed
running from a mob that didn't hear
his silent pleas until his alarmed bigger hastened,   heeding

deformed man   wombs   transformed man

courage   often looks ugly,   to everyone else
but is really,   just   a beautiful thing
living in the courage,   to be yourself

el of all phantasize otherwise
misfits and monsters heroines and heroes alive, even inside
our own bodies   sometimes
window and mirroring societies   ugly beautiful lies,   outside
and beauty full too all the time

rejection deforms acceptance transforms,
that's the treatment—

given unnatural beauty
of living   through both hands
and both minds full of heart   born of it,
manufacturers itself into osseous overgrowth
of by product   being,   you can only
buy   in conformity,
at the price   & cost of humanity,   you can't—

enoch el elephant man,   dehumanizes
thus brother joseph   ain't the one
merrick spoons the medicine
curing everyone,   else   .

mental deforms physical
deformity nurtures, not nature   (under society's spell)
it's mrs kendall
& merrick making alchemy,
in artistic homeopathy
that cures both, of social deformity

it takes an elephant wombed man
to heal   elephant people herded,   like   boxed elephants
who stampede society   abominable   into an overgrown,   hand

boom boom   is both   virus and vaccine,
doctor treves prescribes trial dosage
while doctor merrick   spins up the gene

i've lived this final   scene,
as   31st proverbial momma   saw
my 31st viewing   long ago in a   cosmic magazine?

spectating   the spectacle
of life through   mutating   spectacles
merrick's cathedral, is
momma's   never should of   daring,
to fulfill   & live   our dreams—

single mother build a cathedral
of life's work and service   giving the care
she struggled to receive,   when time came—

boots on at the en,d
good foots scalpeled soul on the mend,

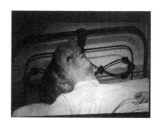

"i heard it" laughter applauds   hereafter,
unlocks placebo memories
to upbraid to up cloud   her resilient elephant,   mane

pillowing legacy   laying to rest
still undergirds   this charioted son's quest,
onward besting   our next tests   here

three-pin-echoing-cosmic momma
sea shells   merrick's refrain,   of   nothing ever dies
still willed   beyond visiting ills   we'll always   rise

nursing kindred   addressing   each other
as doctoring patients   dress   life's wounds
art at life   heals,
as science, too,   repeals
what death walking alive   consumes—

abrahamic treves   and i,
eye mothering merrick   isaac-altered and   hospicing,
from the   contracting rupture of   dimensional door

269

last life breath   given & taken   batons willingly
to finish line   their war,
doctoring   patients   nurse the timeless   cure
elephant sized   hearts, minds, and souls
stampede drum   and trunk up   gabriel trumpet

in love   at
every   life times
horizoning   shore—

13 mar 20

suns raising suns

ray sun
for raising everyone
in,   first—to raise anyone
to raise, another

who can raise shine
sunning others—
raising (best they can) in the sun
twining ones that shine and flower gardens

seed and blossom,
beyond necessary fallowing,
dreams   always in season—

17 may 19

271

rahs jah suns

what happens to a razed city sun
under the feeble shine of a wintry one,
ruth less,   as raisins under guns
and thug life shines, where the man's
shadow allows none—

disappointment's always won?

dreams settle at the bottom,
to compost and fertilize another
icarus or ra jah jump at the heavens—

6 aug 19

272

soular power rememberings

lemongrass shoots stalk tall
peering and leering over
the edge of yellowed cement sidewalk

that maps
foot peddled way
to mrs. monday's   kindergarten—

this sunny day of memory
wears a pastiche fashionable haze
circa 1978,

as the diffused colorful
spring flowers under wind spell
surrounding my youth,   over tell—

nostalgia, suns
every moment lived
from love's photosyntheseismic well

all amounting pays the day

missed takes
mist gives
may bees pollenate,
a life that   just   lives

nectaring sun
seeds possibility's flower
good wiling souls   are yeast of   flour
leavening,   our finest   hours

good giving
nature,   makes mark
in spring   winded   blossomy
applauding,   id—

deeding   dignity
we all   mo' bettering,
dare   have done,   did—

6 aug 19

rune retuning too disney wished upons

palm trees lurch
their dreadlocked fronds
swollen punch drunk by slap boxing
la nina moon tidal waves and winds
toward southpaw stance,

its why these california nights
seem never to end

early am walks
take you back to daytime memories,
where the air you breathe
is the ether you're walking in

bright light theme parks
magnify, under the dense
glass of strip hotels and convention centers
bedazzled and trifoculed by eco-friendly
eyes of translucent bullet buses and uppity ubers,
darting about and around crystalline cathedrals and
metro portals transmuting weekender surburbanites
back into the mere mortality of workaday working folk

every overdose of blinking movement,
each is a wish upon by souls   made   mud full   fleeting stars
that fuels this e-commodizing e-motion towards super
conducted frantic motion—

but stillborn castaways
of ceaseless life,
style in hyper-material
pastiche

congregate as cornerstone
runes meant to re-fork the tune,
as pebbles in the webbing
of mother culture's entangling loom—

homeless souls
yogic, can and do petrify,
making sling shots of their presence
to gentrify,

earth-toned cloaks
dare   ascetically to aesthetic ify
a world built   to commodify

a wishing upon
moving at the light speed
of dreams come always,   true—

gets felled,
by davidic rubble
troubling,
truth out of lies

6 aug 19

275

about moving moments

how many
lifetime's made up
into an infinitely
successive

compilation of movement

go into
the singular moment

when intersecting, intersections
meet?

6 aug 19

grounding macbeth

because

i respect what and how   you dare do

i'll dare what can be, too,
asked of me to
for sake   of a truer,   truth—

living without a   chrysalis stair,
arose within a   castling lair,
whose walls wear   the ear   of speaker & listener,

know to hear
what frankincense anoints   the spiraling air—

this dare
rules the chair
borne with—

crown in, on, and   is

royally stood stool
that, sits—

1 feb 20

twentied verse of us

tuesday school night choice
fated mind change times four,
honoring love's voice —

shadowed silhouette
understood at the spirit
(this) dark mattered reconnect   -tion

as i libated
dance floored moves that pre   stated
2am fog aided

soular conversation —

"just want to ____ yous"
battled "...like you care about   doing, toos"
we stirred,   (e)merging   roux

bathroom nebulized,
i arrived up stairs   you downed
met us (astounded) to meet   our crown

red wine lovers   tip   (stolen)
given   taken,   loving man
floored lover,   took   stand

ruined   wing tips   mapped plan
high street wanderers   hog spit
corner turned   hand & hand —

shampooed improvise
showed and proved true heart wise,
life dance that lied   ahead —

route 3 commutes
met 'she's the one' moments,
you atop your   (universal midnight)   blue

quarter car washed   cavalier   renewed,
bubble bathed and love gum chewed,
rites of passage date taste test   made through,
have always   (never not)   been   loving   (us with)   you —

278

butterflied stomachs in tune,
steeled in the rune of A4's willful door,
you there for me,   among moments   for sure—

misplaced phone calls returned,
scrambled pancakes syruped in loving smiles
'don't gos'   exorcising safety's preserving guile,

wedding planning
and move-in   daze
12 aug '99   photogenic   will always amaze—
buzzing bees held breath,
vows   vowing   vanguard love,
honeymooning   twenty years' long

lived   movie   ing
the real   imperfectly   perfect
always   made   of—

first christmasing
miracle   of what to come
in the moment   we'd made   home,

broken water—

forestalling   made meal prep
36 houring silence   that awaited   rang   loudest ever
kept keeping the sore   unrested   me of us   in step,

for the coming star(s)   been blessed   to accept—

us four moar'd
'kept us keeping on
strong,   from day one—

one day
maybe at 30 years plus
i'll griot on,   this story of us,

this song's   version
sings   proud on,
twenty in,   how it's going on,

a shout   out
reminding us   where
we coming   from—

here,   hear   what words
might could should   rule
this,   poem

look at,   (with)   us
beloved,   since where
we   started   twenty ago—

making our   nonstop   (don't stop)
believing   (in)   is written,
as knowing,   known,   to know on—

279

love you
thank you
for   choosing
yes,   and me,
and   us,
                        eternally—

and stopping
at that bedroom door,
when my   dueling souls
made fuss
of   realizing   destiny,
am still loving   thee   of we   infinitely—

happy twentieth,
                        anniversary!
                                                14 aug 19

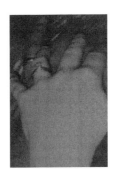

peopling   souls together what things   fell apart

inspired by the proverbs
of chinua achebe's things fall apart

(people made up to be)   things
fall   apart

peopling (souls)   sun
love's tao
to share
in this breakage,
and (worm heavy)   water
soiling compost

as auric
communing atmosphere
that cauls,

placenta
for evolving society
dared be,

to help birth

change—

exiled natives
of one place
claim to become
the nativist exilers of another,

especially
when change
hastens,   things falling   apart—

where seed breaker, is made
among   the broken
by love's cosmic break dancing epic
ritual   all   natural,

locusing manna,

phoenix fire,   ash   fallowing
over-farmed and harvested evil forest,   farms—

for humanist
composting and replenishing

and over
tortoising   time,

this webbed winged falcon of change
and the falconer underneath,
ur-ohm sound keeping time (echoed still now
and always as providential and purposeful)

hear   each   othered   selves'
polyrhythmic tam   taming,
on and of   a widening empathetic

drum—
gathering a together   nest
forged of unique tethers,

drumming totems,
each   us
circling   sankofic away
to oscillate back and forth   anew—

puppets and puppeteers
miming   cosmic   dancing drum,

as living golden ratio
beyond thing,

more peopling
sum   of   some

                              6 sep 19

282

our comings from   is making us   here

waa wah   *equinox*

we all too
make a world   sing resiliency
of   thee
whitman, hughes, angelou   and   me,
for momma jene and uncle t   & e'body, else   come to be—

i am   one   among
in   a long   circling line
of farmers   and teachers
builders   and workers
dreamers and doers

who must too
griot and story sing   here—

art   of life
is where   OHM   coming from
and how   i GOD,   got still   here—

star child of star children
who   keep coming, to dare—

mother's class of '68 waded the waters
of incivility   come to a flood,
father's generation   bled,   all too heavy,   wallace terry's   bloods,

grand father & mother classed   off
becoming bourgeois haves
we weren't,   made of

but kept   laboring   life's laddered loom
to homestead a moveable hearth
in the wages of   hope's   manna—

one   way   ticket
middle passaged
from   southern city   professing   love?

to a more   northern light
where sistren & brethren   might
realize its constitution   at least,   enough—

283

"a boy is born, in hard time   mississippi
surrounded by, four walls that ain't so pretty
his parents give, him love and affection
to keep him strong, movin' in the right direction
living   just enough, just enough for the city"

livin' for the city by stevie wonder

in a prequel
to greater depression
of   social   expressions,

virginian joads and ewells
burned down,   a previously
jim crow   proof   family farm

black wall street   enraged
at just 16 years of age,
grand pop, wielding his granddaddy cain arm,
sounded   an alarm

and had   to be   tom robinson   disarmed—

so family   old school go funded
what might   and   did not remain
to venture capital   us folk
out of   further harm—

and shutter up   for
the coming   market   crash
and   (socio)economic   storm—
we   kept   keeping strong   & moving on

waa wah   my favorite things

my own story,   so far   includes
twenty   plus   life moves
to help   keynesian   prove
home is   wherever   you are

where the atoms   of real life
dare   its smiths   of survival
to melt, bend, morph, and vault
redlining   and   chain ganging   bars—

big banging
ur-own,   hospitable   star—

tiny house
home   steadying
your self, first paying you
just to   furnish and furnace   freidman free   all true
h o l m e s (licensing self)
doing   lived truth,

in one such place
campbell's   & co, souped   up
whitman's beloved camden new jersey
before   its east side federal street   of my time,

284

then social manufactory
mass produced
blight   and flight   by design
as   semantic stew   and rue
to   narrate   native survival
in   mono rhythm   & rhyme —

"don't push me 'cause i'm close to the edge
i'm tryin' not to lose my head
it's like a jungle sometimes
it makes me wonder how i keep from going under"
the message by grandmaster flash

hard working souls
got supped on   to the bone,
half or more of the levitt built row homes
(like too many elsewheres)
turned boarded up skeletons,
decaying down   to the boney   step stone,

had   absentee landlord ships
docked   where   home steadiers
once   stewarded   a sense of   home —

38th & fairmount   next   turned some things around
at u city philly's   black bottom
beneath   the underground,

"do you come from a land down under
where women go and men plunder
can't you hear can't you hear that thunder
you better run you better take cover"   down under by men at work

while its crumbling bricks   and   rear less edifice
angled   the barely livable   third   (among floors)
like a   toppling pyramid   merry go   bound,
we kept it movin   still,   compassed by   & to   a soul ii soul
sound —

"keep   on moving
don't stop (like the hands of time)
click clock   find your own way to stay
the time   will come   someday
why do people   choose to live their lives this way
keep on moving don't stop, no
keep on moving..."
keep on movin' by soul ii soul

u of chi   has got   its south side,
and yale's   new   haven
is   no more   one   for some,   than
paul robeson's princeton   or
dartmouth north   with its shortage
of spry fields and fair views where all peoples'   can reside —

and columbia's village for others,
razed   out of any green (pastures) by soho gentrifying sun,
is   u city penn's mantua mayhem
toughening my part of this   selfsame   town,
visible all the world   around —

285

"so damn tough rock on...
acknowledge my song, bring my posse along
from the heart...my soul.. is in effect...
so i say buddy...study..
dig and learn...dig the move we made...
stunning those who just can't behave...
tough all up in ya...tough crew in effect...
my part of town...so damn tough..."

so damn tough by tough crew

here where   school lunch breakfasts   make for   dinner
and   usda   price fixed   surplus
sweetens up   the   dessert   ed,

fed   self imposed   fasts
fueling   inner gardened   harvests
of doggedly   willed   better life   school workings on
& for   it —

house chores hard knocked ids   out of boredom
as   empty milk gallons always   needed be
hosed full   at the backyard spick,
had us   choosing   what watery
muck   to cook
drink,   wash, or   flush with

call   it
soul   survival   scholarship—

"survival   only the strong can survive
it's called survival   only the strong can survive'
it's call survival in order   to   stay alive
it's called   survival   survival   survival..."
survival by grandmaster flash

street scholars   dodging   drug dealers
and gang bangers,
like sharecroppers   once did
hooded   cross burners   and soul lynchers'   scratching   itches,

we held fast   to our   undeterred
(dreams not to be deferred)dreamer grit—

wicking   (from the inside out)   what
keeps lazarus lady liberty   still stayed woke   & lit
with   all we been about from the real   gitty up   git,

little time   for thebitterness—

"work ourselves,   fingers   to the bone
suck the marrow,   drain   my soul
pay your dues,   and   your debts
pay your respect,   everybody   tells you
you   pay   for   what you get
you   pay   for   what you   get"
pay for what you get by dave matthews band

southwest city upland ave
(near kingsessing)
crowned former pastoral park lands with
graveyard tombstones at mt. moriah near cobb's creek
to foreshadow what meandering migrant   renters' meek
might inherit,   this lifetime, living,   day to day
and at best,   week to week,

286

from   the concrete
and asphalt realm,   too replete
with   pot holes   surrounding —

at   an equator   of opportunity
composted of   difficulty,   abounding —

> "take   that look   of worry
> i'm   an ordinary   man
> they   don't tell me   nothing
> so   i find out   what i can
> there's a fire   that's   been burning
> right   outside my door   i can't see   but i feel   it
> and   it helps   to keep me warm
> so   i   i   don't   mind
> no i   i   don't mind...
> seems   so long   i've been waiting
> still   don't know   what   for
> there's   no point   escaping
> i   don't worry   anymore
> i can't   come out to   find you
> i don't   like to   go outside
> they   can't turn off   my feelings
> like   they're turning off   a light
>
> so take, take   me   home
> 'cause i don't   remember
> take,   take me home"
>
> > take me home by phil collins

john bartram's story
teaches in a way his namesake
neighborhood high school struggled to

as integration's first take
went one way   taking   best students out
but bringing few,   from elsewhere,   in

northeast magnet school
met minds   mining their own   wills   striving,
beyond those   weedy,   concrete covered   land ones
(in the neighborhood)   rigged   already   with   pulled
pins —

i   tested   out
of   masterman's reputation
and   central high's   elocution,
it was   north star at the east   in hybrid   eyes   stationing
of all; as life's   purpose full   vocation,   for me —
stars within   ogled   those   without
making up   spectacles   we could   see,   be —

south west of osage ave not long after   m.o.v.e
got bombed   and   whole street blocks got gone,
making strivers   wonder   what and how   to keep going   on,
will always   be   a apart of where and when i'm coming from
roots footing   the anchor and light house
my i am (ing)   stands on —

3 hour commuter mornings
back to drexel upward bound afternoons,
two a day worknights malling
northeast roosevelt and suburban granite run
and kipelski donut factory weekends
made for monday am   on and on 'til the break of another dawn-—

robbing peters to pay pauls
just enough to forestall
pink slippered landlords
always looming on the next call—

miss meal cramps
purging   school of facts   alone
enlightening lived wisdom's flinty flames
of   ancestors echoing   you're not alones—

same   muse walked senior year   me of us   down
60th & springfield ave to 33rd spruce
and lightless locust walk through windowed houston hall
to get u penn house music'd loose all night long,
then   into basement singing   early morning
my only   s a t   soul striving song—

            "dooh dooh dooh   ah
            oh   the places and spaces   i've been
            dooh dooh   dooh   ah
            oh   the places and spaces   i've   been
            dooh dooh   dooh ah"
                                    places & spaces by donald byrd

supposed to open doors, for
we non-returnables still wading   for,
becoming   necessarily (ourselves),   sanctuary's   shores,
arriving,   just in time,   to show &   hold
        door—

last   drexel upward bound   '91   sprung,
free college applications   with
poems attached that sowed and reaped scholarship,
made basketball swish of pen   as davidic   slung shot,
templelincoln   widener   grossmont
first   generation   to finish, what many dared start—

most thought,   some ball
must   have been   at hand;
yet   on this winged   written prayer

beaconing   life's good fortune
(sala ndege aidan akin)
mine   of us,   still stands—

keyra maasai masai   key of rah,   put   to good use
durojaiye jnani yoga camara   jaiye nan, manifest teacher   of life's truth
sundjiata sankofa ma'at   jah sunning one, who   reconciles us
salajan nsoromashay ashay   winged prayer, phoenixing hope's pixy stardust

jah shaans
and   sala jinns,
help-mating new   horizons
in love's   plowshare, with   my beloved   erin—

288

well, it's not far down   to paradise,   at least it's not   for me
and   if the wind is right   you can sail away   and find tranquility
oh, the canvas   can do miracles, just you wait and see
believe me
it's not far   to never-never land,   no reason   to pretend
and   if the wind is right   you can find the joy   of innocence   again
oh, the canvas   can do miracles, just you wait and see.
believe   me.
sailing   takes me away   to where i've always heard it   could be
and   soon i will be   free

                                                   sailing by christopher cross

1st year college,   cafeteria talk
about   bullets   as seeds
seeds queries   on how to feed
and eat   for a winter on   a $1.25
pocono mountain pete's "buckshot a deer and i bet you'll survive,"

reminds how we found a way too, to get by   on
wish sandwiches, sugar water, and life's coupons,
the world's rinds can taste like thrown stones—
and yet   still keep one
keeping on strong—

each generation before mine (and yours)
gi served and (got) billed
post vietnam still not   40 acre willed
yet   have been,   were willing
to mule bone   still,   here—

    "blackbird   singing in the dead   of night
    take   these broken wings   and   learn to fly
    all   your   life
    you were only waiting   for this moment   to arise
    blackbird   singing in the dead   of night
    take   these sunken eyes   and I   earn to see
    all   your   life
    you were only waiting   for this moment   to be free
    blackbird   fly,   blackbird   fly
    into the light   of a dark black   night"
                blackbird by the beatles

                  (crossfade)

    as   around the sun the earth knows   she's revolving
    and   the rosebuds   know to bloom   In early may
    just as   hate knows love's the cure
    you can   rest your mind   assure
    that I'll   be loving you   always...

    did you know   that true love   asks for   nothing
    no no her acceptance   is the way   we pay
    did you know   that life has given love   a guarantee
    to last through   forever   and another day...

    just as   time knew to move on   since the beginning
    and   the seasons   know exactly   when to change
    just as   kindness   knows no shame
    know   through all   your joy and pain
    that I'll be   loving you
                       always...
                       as by stevie wonder

world made
american   uniquely   inheritor
of dogged, yet not   torn asunder,

striving on
keeping   prize   kept keeping on,
boots   on,   until
wills   done   finished,

story telling, bears   witness—

who i am coming from
and how   here got here   from so far
this is who   we all (each in our own way)   really are
fifty plus one   descendants of cosmic souls   made hopeful guiding stars—

growing up can be a pain
you're not an man until you come of age
we've given up our teenage years
in the effort to pursue our career

who assumes responsibility
of having to support our families
who's protecting us from harm
is there anyone around
that we can trust

so we search for answers to our questions
looking for answers
no answers but we're taught a lesson everytime
through mistakes we've learned to gather wisdom
life's responsibility falls in our hands

keep on learning   keep on growing
'cause wisdom helps us understand
we're maturing   without knowing
these are the
things that change boys to men
                              boys to men by new edition

"ain't nothing gonna break my stride
nobody gonna slow me down, oh no
i got to keep on moving
i'm running and i won't touch ground
nobody gonna slow me down,
oh no, i got to
keep on moving...
                    break my stride by matthew wilder

                        (crossfade)

'i took my love, i took it down
climbed a mountain and I turned around
and i saw my reflection in the snow covered hills
'til the landslide brought me down
oh, mirror in the sky, what is love?
can the child within my heart rise above?
can i sail through the changin' ocean tides?
can i handle the
seasons of my life?   *mmm"*
                    landslide by fleetwood mac

290

so let's   just   listen
to our story   dared, told,   (and live)   within   each other's,   akin
each of us   have and   live   our version   to tell,

some   generation
waded   hosing serpents of   circumstance
hoping to harness,   and water,   sustaining wells,

abdullah   ibrahim
calls   this song we're all on   and among
our waters   from an   ancient   well—

so speak, listen, live, and   hear
each other,   surviving to thrive,   and fill

up   from   enmity's (slavery)
drink, beyond wade,   recycled   muddy   waters
cupping   hard earned   resiliency—

above shame,
libate beloved names
in this life lived   too   you dare proclaim,
to big up   with them   that came (and lived)

so that we could
too   sing an inherited refrain—

and the beat goes on...the beat goes on...
and the beat goes on.. the beat goes on...
bring   that beat back...

resiliency
above shame
is still living
a dared life
we work to live (rather than live to work)   at
maintaining   to sustain—

        "voices inside my   head
        echoes   things   that   they've said"

        house music remix of voices inside my head by sting

play listing & listening
drum circling   each other's   lives
echoes   through   generations
hopes' afloat and   rudder ing,   turning tides,

beating ceaselessly
against all currents   and odds,

in   all of us   gathered,
in & as song   sung & (jacobian ladder) rung   still   here—

                        21 sep 19
                        21 jan 20

291

world tricks, live anyways

the world
might always
try to trick you

always
treat & pay
yourself
first, true
anyways,

momma
used to say—

31 oct 18

we make world economy be sung of thee

remembering   as we for   give
all   of   today   to pay
tomorrow   forward   best we can

we of the world
making it

quarried our backs broke
sung and sing like mined canaries
a dark brightening song through blackened lungs

tracked railroads   bridging continents,
will full   bodies   hammering progress
and   discovering   destiny manifest

like what came of the adventurous
footfalls   of daring natives
wandering across   icy land mass   long ago

where their bean bartered plow shares
became bullion bought time shares
turned fort owned territories
gentrifying these homemade homesteaders
out and beyond walls

we of the world making it up
soonered way west to forge a home,
herded harvests and buffalo

became   them

overseeing reservations of natives we'd later abuse
and plantations of cotton pickers   wed later mass produce

we seamed and steamed
in boxed buildings that dressed to death
are kept still picking through pesticide to   gmo freshness
never needed   apply   unless   our
fire prevention, property protection, or trash collection
gave others   status,   and   rest

we of the world
making it,   come of
and from   debtor castaways
and   so called   fugitive runaways,
darers dreaming   far off away—

chased away potato famines
rooting our hopes   at the bottom
of the white star titans and black star davidians
built on the backs of other barely breaking even blokes,

all ways   suit-casing   hopes—

we   whaled oil
to soul light
compassing through turmoil,

widowing   wives
who lit lighthouses
and made most mo better
of maritime lives

sapped what sap   remained
of our quota mandated   rubber tree bodies
to   good year   our children   with a more cushioned
ride   into next lifetime's   opportunity,

to   guillotine
our   les miserables   difficulty—

stayed   road trip   ready
and traveled   amoebic family
life   of migrancy
to chase down
military   industrial   complexions
of prosperity—

bled   blood diamond   miners
came of   long march, apartheid, pogrom,
and   peculiar   holocaust survivors

arked   yangtze   ganges   nile   amazon
river uprisings

are wealthiest generation
in a long long time   realizers

to what end then,
can   remembering   our stories
add to the dividend of progress
we always   prize on?

we of the world,
making it   what it is and will be,

294

shucked cane
plucked pineapples pined for
fished and fish the seas all too free
workaday grind for less than fifteen an hour

depending on the company   that keeps us
wish to plato's closet all sneakers
thank goodness for toms,
a model for business we might could build upon?

we micro lent before the internet
across differences
in the most turbulent   of times,

built capitol cities   we couldn't yet lead
printed revolutionary times,
lit the world for a fee   and free

we of the world
making it up to be
what it is   and will,   be—

calculated ascent   to moons,
sing now   the story
we inherit   and live   as a most ancient   tune
and embody   its pricelessness,   as a vibrating   rune—

so presently here   together
let's meet the past and future,   we are,
at a gated crossing   the fates   aim to string of our loom,

to condition   change
by   daring   to be
a song   of thee,   among we

in   and beyond,
mere economy

about teaching

understand
what we are doing
so as to celebrate

what is happening

rather than needing
to deter or dismiss
what is

as a teacher
another best year
of teaching and learning
magic—is happening,   again

amidst those, too, scared   to do   growing
beyond instructing   who
beach fowl gather together
as a flock of homing mine miners in suffusing season

but parrot instead,
the muzzling beaking
that aims to weaken the reason,
inner aura purposes teachers to beacon
with fellow porpoises schooling upstream, up-tide,
and counter-current, to   reach us—

arcading the real

while others,
spent spare quarters
on happy meals and arcade marathons

we flipped
heads and tails,
at makeshift bathroom casinos
hoping to pinball enough
to   now & later,   minecraft (on)

twin daze

always been
best friend's friend,
my own twin
from within,
since this when began
until another one,   ends

9 oct 19

wrest love   loving self   among others

"don't have to be a king
to be a king"
j lo

"you're a king,
if you can rule
your own mind"
bb king

you win the race
by walking in your own place—

those picking fights
are   fighting themselves,
got   a lack of   self-wealth—

stop   picking up fights   picking at you   to
pick up   picking on,   too

and love   yourself

as universe
on   purpose,   purposed   you do—

queening   kings
and   kinging   queens
coronates,   even pawns   going thru—

mother   hears
son ask
little big   sister,
now   hefting a hundred pounds,

could she ever
float   or swim her
way   through, wading   heavier   waters?

hurt feels—

filling sibling eyes   and ears,
parenting tongues   wear
just words   about,   just words?

family loving
lives   answers,   flowering   more questions
whose steeped pedals   tea   homeopathic heal ants

how much do you think   i weigh?
daddy weigh?
keyra, mommy,   and sala   one day?

family   plays
about   the mass—

that   strength & beauty,
composting   ugly
thinks alous, as   in love-flavored   stardust

singing life,   makes
of   & in   us   last

10 feb 11
30 oct 19

299

THOU wading through the muck EYES ARE WATCHING hearing speaking glancing GOD
SPARK(S) beyond

"the townspeople bowed down to him because he was all of these things
and yet he was all of these things because they bowed down to him"

                              narrator janie speaking about the townspeople glancing
                              i god-ding mayor starks in zora neale hurston's their eyes were watching god

taboo ifying the language and the accompanying discomfort and violence
associated with   does not erase the reality and experiences surrounding it
nor what it connotes in fact, this can ironically privilege exponentially
micro and macro aggressive social exercises in marginalization this word
can historically name out loud   while muzzling the exorcising power
in linguistically composting language meant to assail   and demean
mere objects   hearing among subjects   saying such signifiers

in a   postmodern   feminist   queer   afam lit theory
way of going through the language of oppressive reality   to get beyond it (repeat)
means all speak   and   all hear   i-it
or hear and speak   the silence choosing   not to   in order to defang   it-it
oppressiveness
and thereby   get   beyond it   ifying dehumanization   of so-called   otherness

all've borne and bear witness—

soul resilient   selves   selfish (in the spirit of preservation)
outwrestle   social caste's   privileges (of expression) by
soul food   i n g,   spoiled projections of   unwanted porridges
laced   with greater   molds   of selfishness—

this   embodiment of being, still here,   business
is   self-evidenced   in all languages
of   experience,
along   dimensional continuums
from utterance   to   silence—

niggardly   nihilistic   namersnobody i n g   way   into some bohdi ness
all ways get   dis   mist   id,

by   phenomenal (phonetic) phoenixes
of nameable and ineffable,   dao pliable   persistence—

                              about the n word
                              eng dept day 30 oct 19

300

story told stores lived manna

"it says here that we are bad
risks and eat up too much of the bread.
we cause bread shortages.
but we only eat our own bread.
 so how can we cause a shortage?"
"...let's put the paper back,
and you can teach me more hungarian."
from aranka siegal's upon the head of the goat

...little chuck little was another member of the population
who didn't know where his next meal was coming from,
but he was a born gentlemen...
jem asked calpurnia to set an extra plate, we had company.
atticus greeted walter and began a discussion
about crops neither jem nor i could follow...
while walter piled food on his plate, he and atticus talked together like two men...
from harper lee's to kill a mockingbird

"my imagination blazed
the sensations the story aroused in me were never to leave me..."
i was afraid that somehow the biscuits might disappear during the night.
I slipped them into my pocket,
not to eat, but to keep
as a bulwark against the possible attack
against hunger..."
from richard wright's black boy

zora had janie
watch   god eyes   watching,
she   of them   had her
glance   with god   in dreamt out   dialogue—

krishna consciousness   in all   its   polyrhythmic
cadences,   builds   companion and relation ships   at a distance,
guy masts   trialogue
made   of   double lived   tetragrammaton   logs—

strung   into   togetherness,
tethering   hulls & sails   loomed
like harmony in   an   anthro-nautical   song,
to siren   wax out of   indifferent ears
and sea shell   all in all of us   to hear

each other   as familiar   shores—

zora had janie
wish on   & live through
coming back   to porch sit   (neighborly) doors

triple time she   was made   to
dream out the   story
life lover   tea cake and she   fished out of
life's   trying   seasons,
fish fried into a   finger fed feast
inside fermenting digestion of life   as a finger lickable yeast
to fuel soular compass   that hopes'   shine and rise on
facing   all ways   inward   east—

these   fish flakes & cakes
wean   them & us   tea caking   jane eyed saris of life (janissaries)
on the stakes of   they & we dare   take in it,

301

making horizon   the tuning fork we ring   and use to hold grapes
just out of wrath's reach,   at a distance,
a fishnet tied   betweening   i (eye) n g(od) us them—

they like all of us,
fly fishing the story of life
by making   icarus flies   atop   daedalus sticks
luring sea yarns   meant to   whale life's tale   with

zora had   other time   selves
chew up   past lived minds   with relish
in the sweet   confectionary of   the kissing-ever-always-young-darkness
while   another time audience   listened in on all this,   a living
story made more alive
she wished on   and dared   live
to   tell;
what is to   tell it   just   to tell on   what was   tole

again & again & again   about existence—

that "you can't buy eyes   in a   store"
be   and exchange the door   plus more   on both sides   of it
you are   already,
wish   making up   real sandwich   in community

life lived
acted on   and done
becomes dreamt truth legal tendered
exchanged as currency   made up to be

conversation as potluck   meal of words
unleavened and leavened in due season
seasoned with purpose,   making bread of story,   too—

seeing (together) makes them (us)these bakers
beyond   gatherers of crumbs   fished into loaves   atop
(thought) otherwise   useless hands, eyes, minds,   lives—

"seeing (ourselves) the woman
as she was (is)
made them (makes us) remember the envy
(and all other feelings informing being human)
they (mirroring us have) had stored up   from other times'

other times' seeing as humanity,
gestates who we will/can be come(s)
and   stored up other times`   insight,
labeled   cans of experience,
stores up   even other times   to sustain this time   and next ones

other times`   see   to eyeing the store
that carrots ours   into mien   (m   i   e   n) minding   a turn with ours
to do the same   for those   beauty eye full not yet   seen borne—

story   pernes
about gyres of   reality
remembers and   re stores identity family   community   society,

302

turns   disfiguring swords
into transfiguring plowshares
sowing sustaining   fruit   of hue and who man   really be
of all   truth,   integrity—

weapon eyed story   of weaponized   kind
laces   its mush   in rumoring gossip   and propaganda
to make   arsenic of elixir   building community
an opiate   of enmity—

now, tool eyed   story
makes plowshare of this sword   in penned and told   word
to break   the petrified ground of fixed mind seht and medusa blocked heart
to bee the buzzzzzz   honeycombing nectar
spread   & come of   gathered nihilism,
in life lived   and fed   from, off, and of the   1 inch deep nitrogen rich

resilient maize   of art   as   edible landscapes—

so called   have nots
have always   had a store
of what can't be   purchased   in one   alone
but rather   in one among   at home,   and belonging

we ourselves cornerstone,
lighthouse lifebuoy, storehouse restore
at the makeshift   crossroads any where   we are together

all owned—

and   so called   haves
have   all ways been   bean stalking
lived memory   that cornerstones
each generation's   pillaring rations   satiating hope's   reason
for remembering   to remember pop up   revelations in inspiration—

of times
when we bartered   experience
as edible   currency
everybody   grew (on)   and had (earned)
and   knew (inside)   as mortaring rue
to makeshift   tabernacle soled   of all souls

home steading meal
supped in & by
the mucky clay of every heel,
of every people's   shoes

once upon   an   every-kind-of-time   lived
to make   sheltering& nourishing   roof   out of every peoples'
mo' bettered   blues

where   stank muck of life   that   (rakes) confines & binds
the   path   our dreams might take,
incasing   our cosmic shine   in the scrap pile of gmo'd faith in it—

303

homemade   rue   of blues
still   always wading   told story   to wade & stir   these quicksands
until time taste tested   compost tastes like generations   ore-ing in story

we   put our collective foots in   with—

story is   soul food   alchemy
of our struggle   to realize dreamt life   beyond reality
& exchange   its recipe   about love
made healing homeopathy

becomes the   zesty (de)fied testified   rinds   (free of binds that
confine)
re-savoring   recipes   of perseverance,
seasoning life's winded stew   of dust bowled dirt
with   our souls   lived grit—

story stores
            stories of us
telling   ours—

this seeds, harvests, barns, and barters
manna from within   we entrust

to pollenate souls' embodying
that   dandelion persistence—
breaking bread   of   as many   bakers
as seers &   livers, actors, and doers   store   urs
stores up   store patrons as seekers
with pantries   kept (in & of them) keeping them   survivors
keepers

feeding all of us as   strivers—

storied word
seeds and feeds   the harvest and hungry

we
store & store up
and must sup to live life   full—

storing story
in the store of life
teaches all   the tao how   of living
as much as feeding   one
                                                    4 dec 19

layering stories

while just
a   few of us   can celebrate
as many as   30 layers of   association gear

or stack   as many oreos
that can tower   and rival sears,

let alone   lego a pyramid
of canned   goodness
to sustain   a deserted neighborhood   of peers—

yet   all   of us,
can ameliorate
as many   chapters   of lived   story
got us   here

like rings   on a   tree
our lives,   echo and vibrate
the trials and exultations   of those
before and after,   rooted and branching,
through the generations   and years—

21 jan 20

we (suns are) be(at) defying drums

we take   drum
and   make drum   up
wherever   we are   (from)
as   we come   (and go)

so   drum
you're vibrating   hum   (ohm)
in   frequent   see,   seas   (seize)   rhythm--

to   sun   on
outside in,   beyond
graying   domes
to   belong,   within   an ozoning one

drummed sun   becomes,
is   home

even among   native
daughters   and   sons,
taking & receiving   drums   in and with them
to vibrate where   belonging   belongs—

circling song, tongues
exchange   lived ryth   hymns
to make up and become,   a new drum sung

for momma jene
on the occasion of your 70 borne day
31 jan 20

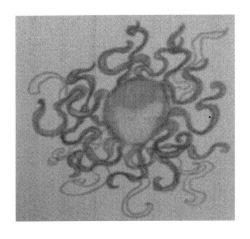

us homing suns are comets eternally spun

home
stays shining
soul

breathing
miniature cosmos
we are,

even when
smog grays over us
with life's grafting bars,

we ray
outside in
anyway,

being this time's
ageless grays,
calls for sages to graze
until the day

sun,
we already from,
comes—

sun home
to big bang
its portable shaan

this homing   in & on,
corner stoning past lives   lived,
brick lays the tiles making aura of roof

as stars
spot, flare, and burst forth
dark matter corona to placenta
life's star dusted truth—

living grays,
suns   alit   without
and those mattering unseen within,

living life
comets us
between them,

guide yours
by your hours,
comet the star(s)
you are

by the push and pull wave
you both ride and spark—

souls are
solars,
cells of galaxies
near and far,

term lights
ant hilling cosmos,
while worm holing counterparts
beneath event horizon,
honeycomb unseen matter—

all us
planets,
begetting comets
inseminating solars
to became stars   are

built of souls,
sunning   love—

outside in
and below, too
as another   above,

all suns   of
cosmos that comes,
radiate and gravitate from
grayed matter within big and small ones—

this home
in journeying, homes
galactic spiraling
super cosmic, multiversal ones   spun

farer and anchor
eternal tether in migration,
sunning comprehension—

31 jan 20

home steady grayed sun

rhyme time
suns,   within

even
its other
more measured kind
grays without (counting beans as coins)
hoop(s) root about time (breaking seeds to beanstalk)

its branches makeup minute hand
to cosmic clock shot clocking
all in all living love @ improvised play
beyond bounds,

to con being and co found
and game time by
working , playing, living this life time
coaching, passing, shooting, fanning, reffing,
hopping, dunking, assisting you balling out you
doing dao yhwh true   anu, anew

31 jan 20

hoop roots hope's memory

those
who know
the hang time
of really getting up,
get down   mad   low
when hoop rising no longer,   can

to really get most high   rep   supped—

hoops' roots
are hopes' memories,
life dared and lived—

as pungent blacktop asphalt,
inherited generational   sense,
retelling lives dared and flung and sung—

stepped back   & forward   crossover,
pot holing ass faults   to vault,

(with) whose   got next
by   slam dunking
balled hopes   in haloed   hoops,

buzzer beating,   this lifetime's   test
in the last breath reflection of winner's,   rest—

31 jan 20

living mamba

redeem the coupon of life
to buy what can't be,
scottie dime your own moses boards
to feed inner mamba kobe

into taking your shot at
living your life, each day   as that

one,   wrist flicked, with
arm, head stayed craned to the sky
and bowed, too, toward i in i

to buzzer beat your win,
outside of shot clocks and time,
until the end—

31 jan 20

compost conformity

i am tired
of people showing me
their ass

trying to shit in my mouth
expecting me
to eat their crap,

like they serving vegetables
they won't accept   from me,

and if
i dare not to eat it
i am somehow showing mine
more than them,

so, i
sustain on my own
what's good
homegrown first,
all life's edible, compost cooked
                    in compost bin,   i am & in

                                        1 jan 20

all eyes gator waders of the see

...”good work, good food
good day, good life...”   —djasahn

dja saans wise sweetening up
our next lunchtime bite,

breaking and being broken
with the land
sweat watering our seeds
sowing hopes, we plant—

all i gator
glancing up
from the muck
is a glance from god i

god eyes
glance up from the mud
as much as down
from the sky

great lake getaway

here one finds inherited hands of earthbound goddess
splaying open upon wavelengths of heavy watery
soul,   light,   and time

at event horizon   portal
of   four elements   congealing
around a fifth one of love,
ash-to-ash stardust   palmed free   below
stokes   lakeshore beguiling star   smiling above—

breath inside dodi dances with winds outside
while tears,   waterfall delta   in rhythm with
great lake getaway train   of heaven-bound, tides—

heart and anchor
cast soul-begetting soul
set sailing, for eternity's ride—

sea shelled   inner ears   conk &   call
this clarion   balloons   sails out of
being funerary   shawl,
for   maiden marital   voyage   beyond time
as   deafening silence tames
all sounds ever   siren sung   to abide—

this   ancestral, celestial   full
faith   wakes, and is   startling
into   living, to become   one—
with   all in all   already   visible
of that which must   leave   to return
what comes back   in new moon tides   arrival
as always,   here   & now—

can hear   the roaring oars   of beloved   gallopers in dance
who mutu   towards   us breaking souls;   being   trans   mutational;
by the wind-driven   watery hands   of see in sea,   (son   ing)
wormhole waves   tam-taming   at the drum   of sun
mirrored   in liquifying   sands—

life lives to take to sea   as   dimensional calypsos   command
all   all ways   brings   back,   as love alive & eternal;   demands,
to the upturned prayerful palm of the welcoming,
volcanic tectonic,   galactic multi-cosmic,   new lands

10 mar 20

wading gathering libation waters

18 jul 20

gateway atlantico

Made in the USA
Middletown, DE
25 February 2021